HOW TO SUCCEED IN THE MUSIC BUSINESS

Wise Publications
New York/London/Sydney

Exclusive distributors:
Music Sales Limited
8/9 Frith Street, London W1V 5TZ, England.
Music Sales Pty, Limited
120 Rothschild Avenue, Rosebery, NSW 2018, Australia.
Music Sales Corporation
225 Park Avenue South, New York, NY 10003, U.S.A.

This book © Copyright 1978 and 1985 by John Underwood and Allan Dann.
First published 1978 by Wise Publications
Revised edition published 1985 by Wise Publications
ISBN 0-86001-454-1
AM19977

Art Direction by Howard Brown
Book Design by Ellen Moorcraft
Illustrations by Gray Joliffe
Typesetting by Letterbox and Capital Setters

Printed in Great Britain by
St Edmundsbury Press Limited, Bury St Edmunds, Suffolk

There are many big names in the music world who, despite all their apparent success, have come out of it with very little to show in the way of financial reward, even though the man in the street may firmly believe that they "must have made a fortune". It is the hasty signing of unfavourable contracts which has been the downfall of many stars.

The temptation is obvious, when you first enter the business, to sign the first piece of paper thrust in front of you, just so that you can wave it about and say "I've been signed up, I've got a record/songwriting contract". This is especially so when the record company or publisher often appears to be doing you a huge favour by "giving you a chance". The days have virtually gone when songwriters would sell hit songs outright for a few pounds, or important artists would make hit records for just the fee paid at the session, but it still can and does happen. The music stars who have succeeded in becoming famous and rich, are the ones who had their heads screwed on.

This book is based on the personal experience of two people who between them have had forty years in the music business. It is not intended to be a definitive work on the subject (such a book would be many times this size and almost unintelligible to most people). Because of this it should not be solely relied upon in place of professional legal advice, for which there is no real substitute in individual cases. It will however help you to avoid many of the most obvious mistakes which are still so common, and it will help you to "have your head screwed on" in the music business.

This book does not presume to teach you how to write a hit song or to sing or to play your instrument; there are however sections giving a guide as to how you can best sell your songs to music publishers and yourself to record companies, pointing out some of the pitfalls.

We strongly urge you to read thoroughly whichever of the following sections is relevant for you, but for quick reference a rough guide to royalty rates and terms offered by publishers, record companies, managers, agents etc. is included in section 6.

Allan Dann was born on Christmas Day in 1949 at Horley, Surrey. He is currently copyright and contracts manager for a leading West End Music Publisher with an index of some 200,000 titles behind his desk. As early as 1959 he began writing songs and in 1963 formed a group, writing and arranging their material. A number of his songs, particularly lyrics, have been published, and his experience in songwriting, performing and recording has proved invaluable in the preparation of this book, enabling him to see many aspects of the business from both sides.

John Underwood was born on 13th May, 1934 in South London. He entered the music business in 1956 as copyright/contracts clerk for a major British music publishing company, later becoming head of that same department. Over the years he has also become concerned with Artist Management, recording, film soundtracks and stage musicals as well as the international music publishing scene, and is now responsible for administration of copyright and contracts for Europe's leading printed music distributor. Both he and his co-author have appeared on national and local radio discussing some of the subjects covered in this book.

CONTENTS

SONGWRITING

RECORDING

ARTIST MANAGEMENT

GENERAL QUESTIONS AND ANSWERS

CONTRACTS

QUICK REFERENCE

SONGWRITING

SELLING YOUR SONGS TO A PUBLISHER

If you have signed a contract as a recording artist with a record company, that company will probably ask for your compositions to be placed with their own publishing company (most of the larger record companies have their own publishing outlets). If this is not the case, then how can you go about deciding which publisher to submit your songs to?

Which publisher should I approach?

The first basic rule is to choose a publisher who is properly in the business of music publishing, and has preferably had at least one or two hits in the recent past. Unfortunately in the UK this virtually rules out any company outside London (or Dublin in Eire), although there are exceptions. In most countries the publishers (and record companies) are grouped fairly closely together in one area of the capital city, the USA being a notable exception with New York, Los Angeles and Nashville (for country music) and other cities being music centres. Most regional publishers are in fact record producers/managers/publishers with the emphasis usually not on the publishing side. For this reason if you assigned your song to even the largest and most reputable of these organisations, the chances are that they would probably re-assign it to a publisher in the capital. So unless the local company is also doing other things for you, you might as well go direct to that publisher yourself. By doing so you will probably end up with a larger share of the earnings and receive any royalties due to you more quickly. A list of publishers with addresses is shown at the end of this section.

How best can I get to see him and put my song across?

If at all possible, try to visit the publisher in person, but do try to make an appointment beforehand, even if you simply phone up asking to come in with your songs in a couple of hours. Sometimes they'll agree to hear them straightaway, unless they are very busy at that particular time. If you wish to sing your song to your own piano accompaniment then tell the publisher beforehand, just in case he doesn't have a piano (some publishers nowadays don't). If you play acoustic guitar it is as well to take one with you. Even a rather poor 'live' performance can often be better than a tape recording, but if you really are not up to performing the song yourself, then better to take a reel-to-reel tape or better still a cassette.

How many songs should I take?

Whichever way you present the songs to a publisher don't expect him to hear more than five at the most at any one time and definitely

put the best one (in your opinion) first. If the first song is poor it's very possible that the others won't be heard at all. If you can, try to make a copy of your tape, in case a publisher wants to 'hang on to it' for someone else in the company to hear. If a publisher says this, don't think that he's intending to steal your songs, but don't be afraid to find out when he'll be prepared to give you a decision on them, and don't be afraid to tell him that if he isn't sure, then you'll simply take the songs elsewhere. Incidentally, don't waste a publisher's time making excuses for the poor quality of your tapes or your voice before playing the songs. Most writers do this but there's really no need. If you're an aspiring singer then the publisher might be interested in you recording for his record company subsidiary (most of the big publishers have these, just as most big record companies have their own publishing affiliates). Otherwise don't worry — it's the songs he's interested in and he'll see beyond your performance.

Is a home-made demo tape adequate?

Naturally a studio-recorded demonstration tape is preferable (see under 'How can I make a demonstration record', Section 2 for details of how to make demonstration tapes) but a clear home-made recording is often adequate for selling a song (much more so than for selling an artist to a record company). A reel-to-reel tape should be at 7½ IPS – inches per second – speed, and should be the only thing on an otherwise blank piece of tape, whether it's recorded on a two or four track tape recorder. You'd be amazed at the number of people who bring in or send in to publishers tapes which are unplayable because there's another song going on backwards on another track.

Is it worthwhile sending songs in?

If you can't get to the capital don't despair. Plenty of songs sent in to publishers from around the country have found their way onto hit records. You should send a tape, addressed to the 'Professional Manager' with a list of the songs and stamps sufficient for the return of the tape if it is not wanted. A copy of the lyrics is also helpful. Even more useful is a top-line (or 'lead-sheet' in America) which is just the words and tune, but this isn't actually necessary. Don't bother to send an accompanying full manuscript with the tape, and certainly don't bother to send in a manuscript on its own. Very few publishers in the pop field will bother to sit down at a piano and assess your song by playing it from a manuscript. If you think the song is suitable for a particular British artist, especially one who has had a hit with one of that publisher's songs before, then there is no harm in suggesting this. Publishers like to have ideas set before them as well as the songs, but be sensible and don't bother to suggest that they

send the songs to Stevie Wonder or Paul McCartney!

How can I find out which publishers specialise in my kind of music?

We have included a list of some publishers who specialise in the pop music field. As with record companies, some are more concerned with soul, country and western, folk, jazz, rock, 'mor' (middle of the road) etc., than others, and the publisher credits on labels of records which you yourself may have will give you a guide. You'll find the publisher's name on a record in tiny print, generally halfway up on the left of the hole on a single, and down at the bottom on an LP. Better still, sheet music will have the British publisher's name usually on the title page at the bottom, plus his address.

Remember that the absence of a publisher's name from this list doesn't necessarily mean you shouldn't deal with him, anymore than the presence of a publisher's name here guarantees his complete competence and integrity etc. Finally a word about publishing subsidiaries. Most publishers have a number of smaller companies which they wholly or partly own. Some of these are simply outlets for the songs of one particular composer, whereby that composer gets a share of the profits on his songs as well as the usual royalties. With a hit or two under your belt you might be offered such a company with one of the big publishers. Because there are so many subsidiaries (one publisher has over fifty) we have only included the most important on this list.

UK MUSIC PUBLISHERS

ATV Music,
19 Upper Brook Street,
London W1.

Ambassador Music,
22 Denmark Street,
London WC2.

Belwin-Mills Music,
250 Purley Way,
Croydon,
Surrey.

Big Ben Music,
18 Lancaster Mews,
London W2.

Black Sheep Music,
Fulmer Gardens House,
Fulmer,
Bucks.

Bocu Music,
1 Wyndham Yard,
Wyndham Place,
London W1.

Boosey & Hawkes Music,
295 Regent Street,
London W1.

Bourne Music,
34-36 Maddox Street,
London W1.

Sydney Bron Music,
100 Chalk Farm Road,
London NW1.

Campbell Connelly & Co.,
8/9 Frith Street,
London W1.

Carlin Music,
14 New Burlington Street,
London W1.

CBS Songs,
3-5 Rathbone Place,
London W1.

Chappell Music,
129 Park Street,
London W1.

Chrysalis Music,
12 Stratford Place,
London W1.

Dick James Music,
James House, Salisbury Place,
Upper Montagu Street, London W1.

EG Music,
63a Kings Road,
London SW3.

EMI Music,
138-140 Charing Cross Road,
London WC2.

Eaton Music,
8 West Eaton Place,
London SW1.

B. Feldman & Co.,
(see EMI)

Francis Day & Hunter,
(see EMI)

Frank Music,
(see Chappell)

Noel Gay Music,
24 Denmark Street,
London WC2.

Tony Hall Group,
9 Carnaby Street,
London W1.

Heath Levy Music,
184-186 Regent Street,
London W1.

Intersong Music,
40 South Audley Street,
London W1.

Island Music,
22 St. Peter's Square,
London W6.

Jobete Music,
23/24 Rathbone Place,
London W1.

Edward Kassner Music,
21 Panton Street,
London SW1.

Keith Prowse Music,
(see EMI)

Latin-American Music,
(see Southern)

Logo Songs,
113-117 Wardour Street,
London W1.

MAM (Music Publishing),
24-25 New Bond Street,
London W1.

MCA Music,
139 Piccadilly,
London W1.

MPL Communications,
1 Soho Square,
London W1.

Magnet Music,
22 York Street,
London W1.

Martin-Coulter Music,
11th Floor,
Alembic House,
93 Albert Embankment,
London SE1.

Morrison Leahy Music,
Flat 3,
1 Hyde Park Place,
London W2.

Pink Floyd Music,
27 Noel Street,
London W1.

RAK Publishing,
42-48 Charlbert Street,
London NW8.

RCA Music,
155-157 Oxford Street,
London W1.

RSO Publishing,
(see Chappell)

Riva Music,
2 New Kings Road,
London SW6.

Rocket Publishing,
125 Kensington High Street,
London W8.

Rondor Music,
10a Parsons Green,
London SW6.

Shapiro Bernstein & Co.,
8/9 Frith Street, London W1.

Sonet Records & Publishing,
121 Ledbury Road,
London W11.

Southern Music,
8 Denmark Street,
London WC2.

State Music,
26-27 Castlereagh Street,
London W1.

Sweet 'n' Sour Songs,
44 Seymour Place,
London W1.

TRO Essex Music,
19/20 Poland Street,
London W1.

United Artists Music,
37 Soho Square,
London W1.

Valentine Music,
7 Garrick Street,
London WC2.

Virgin Music,
95-99 Ladbroke Grove,
London W11.

Warner Bros. Music,
17 Berners Street,
London W1.

Westminster Music,
(see TRO Essex Music).

Williamson Music,
(see Chappell)

Zomba Music,
165 Willesden High Road,
London NW10.

Most music publishers are members of The Music Publishers Association Ltd.,
7th Floor, Kingsway House, 103 Kingsway, London WC2 – telephone (01) 831 7591 –
who can advise of any change of address etc.

PUBLISHERS

Music Publishers have existed for centuries, acquiring manuscripts from composers and printing them for performances at concerts or for sale to the public to sing around the piano at home. In this century however publishing has come to mean finding and then exploiting songs mainly through recording and broadcasting on radio and television. Printing is now a relatively small part of most music publishers' business, and yet many people still imagine that printing is their sole activity.

What should the publisher do for a songwriter?

Generally a publisher will not acquire a song unless he intends to make a top-line copy (tune of the music, chords and lyrics), and a demonstration record (which won't sound as good as an actual record but should be vastly better than you could do yourself). He'll take these around to various record companies to try to get one of their suitable artists to record it. If a record comes out the publisher should help the record company to exploit it, and should print a 'single edition' of it for sale in music shops if it's the 'A' side of a single and looks like being a hit (don't expect him to print it otherwise except perhaps as part of a song book to accompany a best selling LP).

He will then have to deposit copies of the music edition at the British Museum and certain University Libraries (the law demands that absolutely everything printed for sale in Britain be sent to these places). He should also ensure that royalties are collected on the song by notifying certain bodies (see later) and by having it sub-published abroad, so that no money is lost if the song becomes a world-wide hit. He should not charge you for any of this, and should not deduct any of it from your royalties. He takes all the financial risks, but this is what his share of the royalties is for. Beware of advertisements from people offering to publish or record your song for a fee, or write music to your lyrics etc. Only send a song to them as a last resort if no 'proper' music publisher is interested in it but you're really desperate to see it on record or in print. There is nothing automatically bad or crooked about these people. They simply provide a service for a fee, but if you ever hope to make any real money writing songs you will sooner or later have to convince a 'real' publisher that your songs are worth spending money on. Remember there are plenty of publishers around to choose from, none of whom will charge you to place your song with them, nor will they recover any of their expenses from your royalties.

What should the publisher's song contract include?

In principle you'll be selling him your song in return for a purely nominal sum of money (generally 5p) and continuing royalties. If a publisher likes your song enough, he may even offer you a worthwhile sum of money for that song as an 'advance' against royalties, although this is unlikely if you are an unknown. The actual wording of contracts varies a lot, but the royalty terms offered are almost always the same, and even if you are a complete unknown, you should *never* be offered less than the following:

Sheet music (i.e. printed music)

You can expect to get 10% of the actual retail selling price of the music (if it's £1, you'll get 10p). Some contracts allow the publisher to recover the cost of printing the music before paying you anything, and some provide for no royalty to you at all on songbooks or orchestrations, or uses of lyrics without music. You could obviously lose a lot of money through this, and you should try to have such wording removed or altered. On sales of sheet music overseas your publisher will get a royalty which he should share equally with you (this may not be spelled out, but will be covered by the 'miscellaneous income' bit in the contract).

The music edition of a number one in the UK record charts will only sell about 3,000-5,000 generally, as against hundreds of thousands a few decades ago, when sheet music royalties were a songwriter's main source of income. Even today certain songs of the "Imagine"/"My Way"/ "Streets of London"/"Mull of Kintyre" type can sell tens or even hundreds of thousands, but this is quite exceptional. Overseas, sheet music tends to be expensive (often a single edition will be about the same price as a single record) and sales are often very low. Sales of sheet music books on the other hand have never been healthier and the best of these outsell even hit single editions many times over – hence the warning about making sure you get paid on sales of songbooks.

Mechanicals (i.e. record royalties)

You should get at least half the royalties paid to the publisher by record companies for records and tapes of your songs sold in the UK. By law the record companies must pay 6¼% of the recommended retail selling price excluding VAT. So a single which cost £1.50 in a record shop would be about £1.30 with no VAT, and 6¼% of this works out at about 8p. If you wrote one side, you and the publisher would get 4p between you. For LP's and tapes the same formula applies. On a full-price LP selling at say £4.50 including VAT the total royalty would be around 25p, usually, but not necessarily, split into 12½p for each side. The 12½p is then shared equally between all the songs on that side, regardless of how long each one is, and on a normal ten-track LP this gives about 2½p per track (of which you get 1¼p). On a budget singalong LP with about thirty tracks, the royalty would go down to almost nothing, but here the law states that each track must get not less than the 'statutory minimum' of .313p.

If your two-minute song is the only piece of music on what is otherwise purely a 'spoken word' LP, then you and your publisher may well share the entire 6¼% copyright royalty, as the record company will be obliged to pay a separate additional royalty or fee for the use of the spoken material. In Continental-European countries the royalty payable by the record companies to publishers and songwriters is 8% of the retail selling price less tax, but there are provisions for container allowance (deducting the cost of the LP sleeves etc., along with the tax before working out the 8%) and commission deducted by organisations who collect all the royalties from all the record companies on behalf of all the publishers. On balance it is roughly the same as in the UK although, significantly, royalties tend to be lower in the USA where the royalty payable for each musical work on a record rose to 4¼ cents or 0.8 cents per minute (whichever is greater) of playing time in 1983, and these figures are reviewed regularly by a Tribunal.

As regards foreign royalties earned by your song, the foreign publisher usually takes half,

leaving your British publisher with the other half to divide with you, so that you can normally expect to get a quarter of the total royalty payable on the song overseas. This might seem unfair on you, but it's quite normal.

None of these royalties may seem very high and in particular the minimum, .313p is laughably small. When this was introduced as three farthings in old money (0.313p is the new pence equivalent) it represented one-half or thereabouts of the normal royalty. Today it is more like one-seventh! A revision of this in conjunction with the 6¼% basic is long overdue. So don't think your publisher is swindling you if you only get 2p per record for a smash Top 10 UK hit. It will have sold about 200,000 to get there anyway, which means you'll still end up with £4,000 from the hit recording alone and there may well be other royalties from two or three cover versions (cheap LP's of hits selling in chain stores, at garages etc.) all of which is not to be sneezed at.

PRS (i.e. performance royalties)

The Performing Right Society Ltd (PRS) was founded in 1914 by composers, songwriters and publishers to protect the performing and broadcasting rights in their works by ensuring that appropriate royalties are paid for all broadcasts and public performances of music. The PRS makes a charge to every dance hall, club, pub, restaurant, record shop etc. in the country if it wishes music to be publicly performed on its premises. In principle all these places should send to the PRS a list of every song performed there during the year. In practice, neither the majority of the places licensed nor the PRS itself has time to analyse this thoroughly, so samples are taken and in effect the vast majority are assumed to have used the usual big standards plus the year's chart entries. On top of this, the PRS collects lump sums from the BBC and IBA for broadcasting music on television and radio. The PRS then shares out all the money collected that year amongst all the songs used. The size of the share is related to the importance of the performance. The big money comes from television and radio broadcasts – less then £1 per song on some local radio to several £'s or more for Radio 1, 2, 3 and 4 and tens of £'s for a networked television performance. You get slightly more if the song is "featured" (apparently being heard by the people on the screen) than if it is "background".

If your song is broadcast on television or on Radio 1, 2, 3 or 4 then you can definitely expect to be paid sooner or later. However, with local BBC and independent radio stations in the U.K. PRS find it almost impossible, as they do with the "returns" of songs from the disco's etc. to keep track of every use of every song played, and they base their payments on a sampling system. Of course the staff and running costs of the PRS (in spite of computers) would increase enormously if they were to analyse all returns. However it is very bad luck for a composer who has had lots of plays of his song on one or two local radio stations to find that he gets nothing at all because his song was not in the sampling. Radio Luxembourg, although heard across Europe, is treated as a local Luxembourg radio station and the fees, which are consequently very small, are collected from French "Society" SACEM by the PRS in respect of British songs, and if you are not a member of PRS or any of its foreign equivalents then you won't collect anything from Radio Luxembourg.

If you are not a member of the PRS then the PRS will pay all the fees they are able to collect on your song to your publisher who will pay your share of them to you under your contract with him. It will never be less than half for performances in the U.K. because the PRS will pay out in accordance with a notification card which the publisher prepares and must ask you to sign. Have no fears about signing this because the PRS simply will not accept it if it should state that the composers and authors between them will receive less than 50% or six-twelfths of U.K. earnings (the PRS deal in twelfths for convenience). The rules of the PRS state that the writers should receive 8/12ths. and the publisher only 4/12ths. unless they have evidence (the notification card or a copy of your signed contract with the publisher) that you have agreed to 6/12ths.

Can I and should I join the Performing Right Society?

A publisher must be a member of a Performing Right Society (the PRS being the British society) to collect all his performing fees, but a writer can also join even if only 3 of his songs have been publicly performed. It is clearly a waste of your time and theirs to apply to join PRS if your songs are not being used, nevertheless if you are having any activity on songs you should join without delay. There is no subscription and we would strongly urge any British writer to join PRS, for not only will you be paid directly by them and therefore more quickly than if the money had to go via your publisher, but also you will be paid certain royalties from abroad which not even your publisher could collect for you all the time you are a so-called 'non-member'. To join, simply write to 'The Registrar, the PRS, 29/33 Berners Street, London W1' asking for the relevant forms, and these will be sent. There are no charges of any kind and you can only gain by it. As regards foreign performance royalties, the publisher finds himself sharing his part of these with a foreign publisher, and sometimes the same applies to the writer, who has to share his part with the writer of the foreign lyric in each country, usually to the extent of 1/3rd. him, 2/3rds. you, even though the big money in foreign countries may be earned without the foreign lyric actually being used a great deal. This may seem unfair but don't blame your publisher or the PRS as there's little at present that they can do about it.

As you will have gathered, all your performance and broadcasting royalties from the U.K. and around the world will come to you automatically once you are a member through the PRS. As a member you will receive regular bulletins and reports which are well worth taking the time to read, about the work of the PRS and its foreign affiliates. This work includes efforts to protect and increase the rights of British writers in many overseas countries and in new areas of technology such as satellite and cable television, as well as supporting British musical institutions, organising additional benefits for its members, sponsoring competitions etc. As a PRS member it is in your interest to keep a detailed note of broadcasts of your songs as this will assist the PRS in ensuring that you are credited with royalties earned.

Are there any other sources of income and what should my share be?

Miscellaneous (usually half of everything else the publisher receives on a song)

This section includes foreign sheet music royalties as we said earlier. More important it includes money which the publisher charges for allowing the use of your song in a film or television commercial. This can be a great deal of money in the case of a hit song or a standard which is used in a major film and often several thousand pounds for a nationwide television commercial and you will be paid half of this fee provided that film or advertisement was made and licensed in the UK. If it was licensed abroad then your publisher will be paid a proportion of the fee which the foreign publisher charges, and again you will get half of whatever your publisher gets. Remember that if your song is unimportant or has ceased to earn very much money a publisher may charge a low fee at his discretion, just to ensure that your song is used and not substituted by another. This is because he may wish to regenerate interest and activity on your song, and because in any case whenever and wherever the film or advertisement which includes it is shown, a performing fee will generally be payable to the benefit of both of you.

There are also smaller fees obtainable for the use of your song in radio commercials, private documentary films, stage shows etc., (see also under Q. & A. 'films, musicals and plays'). Your publisher will also extract fees for the use of songs or song lyrics in books, newspapers and magazines. Around £150 is often obtained for a hit lyric in a magazine. From all these sources of income, your publisher pays at least half of what he gets.

How often will I be paid ?

It is customary for a publisher to pay composers twice yearly, a certain number of days (usually 45-60) after 30th June and 31st December every year. Generally if no money is due to you a blank statement should be sent, but often is not. Check your statement to see that any large sums which you expect to be there are not missing, but remember that money takes a long time to reach you from the time when it was first earned (explained in more detail in 'General Q's and A's later on).

The PRS distributes fees four times per year. Basically two accountings for broadcasting (UK radio and television) and two 'general' (samplings of concerts, disco's etc.) plus foreign royalties.

What if I only write lyrics?

It may be that any strength in your songs is with your words rather than your music. Very few individuals are really strong in both. The music generally has all the emphasis and the words can, even in a hit song, be quite inane and on recordings often inaudible anyway. It is fair to say that many composers spend very little time on the words concentrating instead on the all important 'catchy melody'. Words can however also be the making of a song and if you are told your songs are musically weak, don't despair. It is quite possible to find another song-writer who has good musical ideas but is quite unable to 'put two words together' as it were, or who works better if supplied with title and lyric ideas to start with. As a rule, if you collaborate with another right from the start then you are both treated equally when it comes to dividing royalties and fees. Another source of work and income for a good lyric writer is the putting of words to foreign songs for the English-speaking market. You do not have to have knowledge of the original language (unless of course the publisher particularly wants the theme of the original lyric preserved). Many of today's great songs originated in South America or on the Continent and it is the work of the USA or British lyric writer which has contributed to some extent to their acceptance by our public.

As we said earlier you as a UK writer would lose two-twelfths out of the six-twelfths writers share of performing fees abroad to a foreign lyric writer. Thus this is what you should get for writing an English lyric to a foreign song, although this won't be spelled out. The term in the publisher's contract 'in accordance with the rules of PRS' will cover this division, and you won't be asked to sign a notification card. Only the publisher need do this for foreign original songs. On record royalties the usual percentage offered is 12½%, as against 50% on a normal song writing contract, although as much as 15% or 20% is paid to top lyric writers, and 10% is still quite reasonable. Avoid giving your lyric the same title as the original song as it is unfair to expect bodies collecting royalties to differentiate between uses of the song with or without your lyric. UK sheet music royalties will usually be 2½% of the retail selling price (as against 10% if you wrote the whole song). This sounds terribly low when converted into cash, but is quite normal.

Will I collect on all uses of my lyric to a foreign song?

Surprisingly the answer is no. In a few countries your lyric will still be disregarded when it comes to making mechanical (record) royalty and peforming royalty distributions. Some of the societies administering the distribution of fees are very nationalistic and they refuse to accept that records are sold and performances take place in their countries of anything except the local language version. As a consequence even if you know and can prove that records reproducing your lyric have sold in a particular country the person actually receiving the 'lyric writer share' may be the local writer. Only if a lyric in the language of the country has not been produced do you stand a chance of participating and that will be because the publisher on the spot will receive in effect 100% and provided that he has acquired rights to your lyric from your publisher then astute accounting can result in your receiving monies earned. You will appreciate however that in the first instance the original publisher, (let's say for example it is a French song to which you have written a lyric) may have given rights to all sorts of publishers in various countries none of whom have direct relations with each other. The British publisher who acquired your lyric may have rights for the UK and Eire only and therefore its use in Germany is by a contract between the French original publisher and the German sub-publisher and it's difficult to fit you into that scene. In theory the rights to your English words will go to the German publisher via the original (French) publisher, but so will the rights to Italian, Spanish, Swedish etc., etc., lyrics and so it is perhaps an onerous task for the local collecting society on the spot to sort out just what version has been played or recorded, hence the easy way out, assume always it is the local version. A current way of tackling this is for you, the lyric writer, to withhold from the British publisher rights to your lyric outside his territory. If he's only got UK and Eire in the music then only give him UK and Eire in your lyric, leaving yourself free to try and do a deal with the foreign publishers controlling the original composition. In some countries the PRS is endeavouring to collect a share for a member who is a British sub-lyricist in cases where his lyric is quite clearly being performed.

What about all the other small print?

Apart from the royalty clauses there will be a clause in which you guarantee that the song is 'all your own work'. As you are technically selling the song to the publisher in exchange for a sum of money, however nominal, the publisher has the right to take you to court if he ends up out of pocket because the song was in fact not all your original work. In practice of course this doesn't happen, as he's on your side, but it's a good reason to make quite sure that your songs really are original. The contract will also state that the publisher is appointed to act for you should someone else try to claim your song, infringe it, or use it unlawfully.

The publisher also acquires the right to have new lyrics made, in the UK and abroad. Morally he would be wrong to change your English lyric, although he might ask your permission to make substantial changes to the original English lyric, or the title, or the structure (verse, middle "8" etc.) if he really thought it would improve the song. Generally he would tell you all this right at the start, often before you had even assigned the song to him. He would normally ask you yourself to rewrite any parts he felt needed improvement before resorting to anyone else.

If the publisher wishes to pay royalties to anyone else for partly rewriting your song he should do so out of his own share of royalties and fees, and yours should remain unchanged. If the song really is drastically changed and improved by a new writer then the publisher may ask you to share part of your royalty with the new writer. This is quite reasonable provided that the changes are substantial and, to your mind, an improvement. Alterations are quite frequently suggested and made by the publisher's promotion staff with no suggestion that they become, in effect, part-writers with a credit and a royalty.

If you do feel however that you are being pressurised into cutting someone else in on a song for no good reason then simply refuse to part with any of your shares on that song and take your future compositions elsewhere.

If your publisher should tell you that he can secure a recording of your song on the A-side of the next single by a major artist and established hitmaker on condition that the publisher parts up with a small percentage of the publishing royalties on that record, again he may ask you to bear part of this, and again this is not unreasonable, though if you do feel strongly about it, remember you are not obliged to say yes. An arranger in the UK does not receive royalties when he makes an arrangement of your composition (although this does happen on the Continent, and your share of performing fees may thereby be diminished), see also under 'Can I and should I join PRS'.

COPYRIGHT (FOR SONGWRITERS)

This began centuries ago as simply the right to make copies for a limited period. Since that time it has been expanded to include the right to perform a song in public, grant permission for its use in films etc., make records of it for sale to the public and so on. In the UK two major Copyright Acts, in 1911 and 1956, form the basis on which most of a songwriter's rights rest. By various international agreements, notably two events called the Berne Convention and the Universal Copyright Convention, your song, whether written in the UK or elsewhere, is protected to a greater or lesser extent in almost every other country of the world, although there are exceptions. Most of these countries have also passed various Copyright Acts during this century, updating the law to cover the new discoveries in which music could be used, such as records and tapes, radio, T.V., films etc.

How do I copyright a song?

In Britain you don't have to do anything to 'copyright' a song. As soon as it actually exists outside your mind in some 'tangible form', that is once you have written it down or made a recording whether amateur or professional, then technically copyright begins from that moment. It is the same in many other countries, although in the USA the system has long been for it to be necessary to 'register' songs in the copyright office in Washington and to pay a fee of a few dollars.

The international symbol of copyright is a 'c' in a circle ' © ' and if you are sending or taking around manuscripts or lyrics with tapes of your songs you should write, at the foot of the first page of any manuscript or lyric (c) copyright by . . . (your name and address).

In the UK even if you sell your song to a publisher, you are the first owner of the copyright, and in some continental countries you always remain the owner and in effect you only license the publisher to do certain things for you i.e., print, collect royalties etc. The only time in the UK when you are not the first owner of a copyright is if you were employed by someone else to create it, as with a newspaper reporter writing an article.

How long does copyright last?

The exact time of creation of each song is not important in the UK, as copyright lasts for the whole of your lifetime and for fifty years after that. If two of you wrote the song together then copyright continues for fifty years after the death of whoever dies last. This is not too likely to worry you, but might concern your heirs. Thanks to the international agreements we mentioned earlier this applies in the UK to foreign songs as well, and your song will in turn be protected for the same or roughly the same length of time in most other countries too, including (from 1st January 1978) the USA, where until recently the rights only lasted for a total of fifty-six years.

What if someone steals my song?

If you heard a song in the charts that sounded exactly like one which you wrote say a year ago, you would have to prove that the writer of the hit 'had had access' to your song i.e., had had the opportunity to hear it, and then copy it. If you kept the song to yourself and the only copy was in a self-addressed registered envelope, or in a Solicitor's or Bank Manager's safe keeping, which are two processes often suggested to new composers, then 'access' would be impossible and the similarity in songs would be regarded by the courts as coincidence. By sending a tape or manuscript of it to yourself in a registered envelope left unopened and intact, you could at least prove that you hadn't stolen the hit, by establishing that you had written your song long before you could have possibly heard the hit, but now no publisher would be interested in it and you'd have to write it off as very bad luck. If you really thought a song of yours that had had 'exposure' had been stolen, and, perhaps surprisingly, it happens very rarely, then your publisher would take up the matter for you. George Harrison's "My Sweet Lord" is the only example in recent years of an 'infringement' of one song by another song which has been seriously challenged in the courts.

BLANKET WRITING AGREEMENTS

Most publishers who think your songs have any promise will want to give you a 'blanket' songwriting contract for a period of years, so that if they've spent a lot of time and trouble and money trying to promote your earlier efforts, they're guaranteed your entire output at least for a while once you've started writing hits. The British Courts of Justice don't look too kindly on 'exclusive' agreements for long periods which appear heavily loaded in favour of the publisher. They say that they could be restricting the development of your career, and for this reason any British publisher trying to sign you up for more than five years is probably making his contract unenforceable should you wish to take your songs elsewhere for any reason.

What if the publisher wants to sign me up?

The ideal blanket agreement will be for one year with two options for the publisher to renew it, each for one or two years, making three or five years altogether, although a straight three years would not be unreasonable.

By signing it, you will be giving or agreeing to give to the publisher all the songs that you write during that time. Obviously the publisher may think (so might you) that some of the songs are totally uncommercial. Most, but not all, publishers will give you back the rights to the songs which you think are good but which they don't — if you ask for them, but it is better to have some provision for returning the 'dead' songs to you written into the contract. Incidentally if you also write books or poetry for a book publisher, be sure that the wording of the music publisher's contract leaves you free to do this.

Why sign a blanket agreement anyway?

You may well ask what is the benefit to you in agreeing to write exclusively for one publisher — why not leave your options open to write for whoever offers you the best deal? The usual inducement is money. The publisher may offer an advance payment which he can recover from your royalties but which he can never make you pay back even if at the end of the contract none of your songs has earned a penny. Another reason to sign is that it may encourage him to make much greater effort in promoting and developing your career if guaranteed all your songs for a certain period, as he has a vested interest in a part of your future. He may simply suggest that everybody does it and that he isn't interested in you if you don't sign exclusively. Be wary of this, although by all means sign if you really want to, but not for more than one year with a provision for him to pay you an advance payment at the end of that year if he wants to keep you any longer, unless of course you are both quite happy after one year in which case the contract can be extended by mutual agreement.

How would I get out of a blanket writing agreement?

The first thing you do is simply write to the publisher asking for a release. He'll probably be quite prepared to do this if he's having no success with your songs, or if you have any justifiable grounds for being discontented with him, or if you really have virtually stopped writing. If he paid you a large advance royalty sum which shows no sign of being recovered by him, he may offer to release you from the contract provided that you refund to him part of the advance. This is reasonable although he should give you back the rights to the songs you wrote under the agreement if he expects you to pay back all the advance which he hasn't already recovered. If he won't release you, check through your royalty statements for accuracy and regularity. As we have said the contract will normally provide for these to be sent every six months, so many days after 30th June and 31st December. If they are not being sent on time then write to the publisher demanding that he keep to the terms of the contract. If he continues not to account to you monies due, then you have grounds for termination. If the contract only requires royalties to be sent to you 'as soon as possible' after 30th June and 31st December this should still not be more than about three months after each of these dates, though of course no-one can actually say what's 'possible'. Also check any renewal. If he hasn't renewed on time, then you're free (provided you haven't been continuing to give him songs as though the contract were still in force). If you feel you need to start writing 'threatening letters', then get a solicitor to do it, but always start with the friendly reasonable approach, and remember that one default in royalty statements is not grounds for you simply to go elsewhere, the default must be persistent. Incidentally there's no point in writing for another publisher under a pseudonym. You'll have to tell PRS if you want your performing fees and they'll say "Sorry we can't register this. If you're really Fred Smith then you're under contract to so and so" (they don't take sides, but they do have all this information stored up).

Can I cut out the publisher and collect all the money myself?

If you have the contacts and time to fix recordings and promotion on your own songs, you may well wonder why you should give 50% of your earnings to a publisher. Obviously you will need to be a member of the PRS to collect your performing fees. You'll also need to have some means of collecting money from record companies, as it's virtually impossible to collect from them all individually. This means joining another important body in the music business which we have, so far, not mentioned, the MCPS (Mechanical Copyright Protection Society Ltd.) or, alternatively, one of the two or three much smaller concerns which also offer to collect your royalties for you. Based in Streatham, London SW16, the MCPS collects money from UK record companies, chasing them up and prosecuting them if they don't pay. Incidentally MCPS also licenses and collects fees for songs used in films, discussed by us earlier, and performs a host of related tasks such as charging record shops royalties for importing records, prosecuting bootleggers etc., all of which as you can imagine is an enormous task. MCPS then pays out the money it has collected to the appropriate publishers (or composers) after deducting a small rate of commission. Unlike the PRS, not all publishers or composers do in fact use MCPS's services. Through MCPS you would of course get around 90% of the total record royalties which your song earns in the UK, instead of 50% of the total collected by your publisher direct from a record company (or slightly less in effect, on money which your publisher may himself have collected from MCPS, less commission) but against this you lose the exploitation and personal attention to your song which you would expect to get from a publisher and if you want to meet a demand for music editions then you will have to have the song printed at your expense. Overseas you would be in danger of losing large sums of money, as only the foreign associates of PRS and MCPS would be looking after your song and they would be unable to make foreign lyrics, chase up illegal users or infringers, promote, print or fix recordings etc.

GENERAL QUESTIONS AND ANSWERS ON SONGWRITING

Are the BBC and IBA important?

Yes. Like all loving aunties, the Beeb and commercial radio and television have soft spots for the young and can provide help in the form of a leg up the ladder. The producers of many programmes, particularly in the children's, religious and chat show fields are always in search of new songs and music for use in their shows and you can send in tapes and ask for an appointment just as you would to a music publisher. Addresses are given in Section 6. The names of individual producers can be found from *Radio Times* and *TV Times* or from screen credits.

Don't neglect schools' radio programmes and television children's shows which generally feature music. In the course of a year, such shows consume literally hundreds of songs, many of them commissioned from new, up and coming songwriters. The BBC's children's shows employ excellent singers, including often future stars, and a song or piece of music performed on one of these shows is a very nice credit. Schools' radio also consumes a lot of material and some very good songs have been commissioned by schools producers and performed by well known artists and groups.

How do you find out what is required? First of all, spend a few hours listening to output and

getting the feel of what is being used. On the television front, nationally and locally there are opportunities, particularly as there are now four channels in the U.K. Together with breakfast television and the emergence of cable and satellite television all of these developments mean that more and more programmes are being made, many by independent film and production companies who have contracts to supply programmes to the television stations, and here again music is certain to be used to some extent. As it can be costly for producers of these programmes to use existing successful songs in them, this is an incentive for them to commission new specially-composed music. It is now possible to produce a competent video on quite a low budget, suitable for some local television slots, and this sort of thing could provide a good opportunity for a new songwriter.

If you are successful in interesting the BBC or Independent Radio or TV in some of your music, they will wish to acquire world broadcasting rights in it. This is so they can sell the programme all round the world without prior reference to, or permission from you, although you would of course still get broadcasting fees in all the places where the programme was shown or heard. In practice they will be content to accept just broadcasting rights from you, leaving you free to assign all the remaining rights, performing, recording, printing etc., to a publisher. If you get to know the people concerned with certain television programmes they may commission you to write specially for them (e.g. theme music), but here again you need not necessarily part up with more than just broadcasting rights in respect of a particular programme.

Can I or my publisher stop anyone recording my song?

As a preface to this answer, remember that once you have assigned the copyright in your song to a publisher, then although he may wish to consult with you, the song is nevertheless legally his property, and any restraint on the use of the song is really entirely at his discretion.

Your publisher can prevent a recording being released in the UK provided that no recordings of that song have been released in Britain before. If for instance your own group's record of a brand new song is to be released on a certain date and you wish to prevent competition from another record company's version, then your publisher may place a so-called 'mechanical restriction' on the song, by notifying the record companies that they may not bring out a record of it before a certain date (i.e. the date your record is to be released). Once your record is released however then any other company can release their version at any time afterwards, or even on the same date, and you can do nothing to stop them, although they do of course have to tell your publisher beforehand that they intend to record the song and they have to pay the 6¼ % royalty.

Can I or my publisher stop anyone else performing my song?

As regards performances it is virtually impossible to prevent people performing your song before a certain date once they have been able to get hold of some material (sheet music, demo tapes etc.) from which to learn it. Once the song is well-known then a performance can only be prevented if for instance it is a parody or is included in a film or show without having been properly licensed. In most cases an unwanted performance is of no great consequence. Only in the case of a song contest entry where all the songs must be entirely new and unheard by the general public is this likely to become important.

Can I or my publisher stop anyone else printing my song?

Anyone wishing to print the song in any form will have to apply for permission to the publisher, although British Copyright Law does provide that very small extracts may be quoted in magazines and newspaper articles etc., (though not in advertisements) without a payment or credit being made. It is of course impossible to say exactly when a small extract becomes a large one but generally three or four lines is the most that could be regarded as permissible.

Can I or my publisher stop anyone making a parody of my song?

The answer is yes, although this does sometimes happen without your prior knowledge. Generally parodies do not really 'damage' a song, even if the parody is used in a big television commercial extolling the virtues of toilet rolls. A parody should be cleared specially with your publisher by the user before it is used, and the parody writer should never receive a written credit or part of the royalties. Few writers complain (unless they consider their songs to be highly poetical) as recorded parodies are often big sellers.

What happens if my songs are included in Musicals, Plays and Films?

Unless this has come about through your writing music for the BBC or an independent television company then it isn't likely that you'll be asked to write the score for a television programme, film or musical until you're well established in the music business. If this happens with a musical or a play, the producer will usually pay you a fee in return for the 'grand rights' to your music. There is actually no definition in law of grand rights but in practice they are regarded as the right to use the music in a dramatic performance in costume (i.e. a live stage show or televison version of the same). The fee may be a share of the box office receipts from theatres staging the show. You should not give a producer any other rights as these can be given in the normal way to your publisher.

If a few of your songs are incorporated in a musical then your publisher or the PRS may charge a fee for each performance or run of performances, and this will take the place of a much smaller ordinary performing fee which would otherwise have been payable. Most publishers would regard it as petty and uncharitable to exact a fee for the use of a song or two in a local primary school Christmas pantomime, but the fee for their use in a big West End production could be tens of pounds every week.

With films your publisher will exact a synchronisation fee for the initial inclusion of your music in the film and you will also receive ordinary performing fees when the film is shown in cinemas or on television.

If I write a song with someone else how is the money divided?

Probably the majority of pop songwriters in fact write in teams, usually two, often one supplying the ideas and lyrics and one supplying the music. Members of a group, however many in number, often write songs together for LP's and B-sides of singles. If you and let us say one partner jointly write a song and are shown on the contract and the PRS notification white card as joint composers and authors then you will each get an equal share of the performing fees. As regards record royalties etc., if both your names are on the contract with the publisher then regardless of how much of the song each of you actually wrote, the publisher will divide the record royalties, sheet music royalties and other royalties equally between you.

If you wish to vary this straightforward division so that one writer gets more than another then you will have to let your publisher know before he prepares the contract and the white card, as the agreed shares will have to be set out on both.

Bear in mind that although publishers will usually go along with your variations in these divisions such variations are headaches for accountants and you will not be too popular if you continually ask to have the shares divided in exactly the same proportions as your respective contributions to the songs. Most writing teams simply split the royalties on every song in which they each had a hand equally between them. In the case of performing fees these are always spelled out anyway on the white notification card. The total writers' share is usually six-twelfths and any division of this ought to be in whole twelfths and not fractions of twelfths.

Something else to bear in mind is that an agreement is not valid unless it is signed by all the parties to it. This means that if a publisher sends to you and your partners several copies of a contract for a song it is of no use for you each to sign one copy before returning it — dreary as it may seem, you will all have to sign every copy.

If you write the music and your partner the words to a song, then you are both in effect 'original creators' of the song, and you will both be paid on all uses of it, even the words on their own and the music on its own. If on the other hand someone else came along later and added a lyric to an already existing instrumental of yours, then he would be entitled to receive fees for the use of the tune with the lyric and for the lyric alone, but not for performances or recordings of the instrumental version under its original title. Ideally his title should be different from your original one or he may collect incorrectly on performances of the instrumental version. The PRS do endeavour to establish whether performances are vocal or instrumental versions of the same song, but if the title is exactly the same

then this naturally makes things very difficult for them.

What do I get when my music is hired out?

This will generally come under the 'miscellaneous' section of the contract, and you will get 50% of whatever the hire fees amount to on your music editions (generally only serious music, symphonic works, classical pieces or the scores of musicals are hired out). This is fine if it is your publisher or someone licensed by him who is doing the hiring. You have probably hired musical equipment or a car for a short period of time, and it will be no surprise to you that the makers of the equipment, or car, did not receive a cut of the fee you paid for the hire. Upon this same principle there is a small but rewarding business run by some publishers in hiring out other publishers' music. Your publisher may sell an edition for say £5, whereas another publisher will buy a copy and re-offer it for hire at £2 per month. Someone wanting to perform the composition for a short time and perhaps operating on a small budget (a school orchestra for example) is quite likely to hire rather than buy, so that you and your publisher lose out. Although it is not illegal it seems altogether morally wrong that some otherwise reputable music publishers should engage in this business in the knowledge that no part of the fee they obtain is payable to the composer or original publisher, but that's the way it is.

Can I use bits of other peoples songs in mine?

No, this is an infringement of someone else's copyright and he could sue you. Such uses do happen especially by jazz musicians who are adept at putting snatches of completely different songs into their variations on the particular song that they're playing. You'd be very silly to write a song incorporating part of another song unless it was a 'traditional' one (see next section for explanation of traditional songs). The reason for this is that provided any piece of another song can be identified in your song as being definitely recognisable (even one line), then the composer and publisher of the other song can claim half(!) of all record royalties on your song, if it's on a single, on the grounds that there are in fact two songs reproduced, not one. On an LP you lose out too, but to a lesser extent as there is in effect another song on that record which has to share the royalty payable for the appropriate record side. In the USA things are slightly different, in that a certain number of bars have to be identical before the other publisher and composer can step in and make a claim. It all may seem very unfair, but the only way out is to ensure that no part of any song of yours is lifted from some other song.

Will I be paid on my versions of existing songs?

This depends upon whether or not the existing song which you want to rearrange is 'traditional', which is simply one of the words describing a song whose writer has been dead for over fifty years (copyright in songs remember lasts for the writer's lifetime plus fifty years after his death). If the song is traditional then your new arrangement of it, even if you've hardly changed it at all, becomes a new copyright (expiring fifty years after your own death) and the publisher and record companies will pay you on it just as if it were all your own work. The PRS on the other hand have a system whereby what is called a 'music classification committee' reads through manuscripts etc., of songs notified to them as arrangements of traditional works. These arrangements are then 'downgraded' according to the amount of new material there is in them. An arrangement which sounds just like everyone else's (i.e. just like the original, if

indeed it's known what that really sounded like) may only be allocated three-twelfths altogether, instead of twelve-twelfths. Where the entire song has been drastically altered, perhaps with new words, as much as nine-twelfths may be allocated.

As you can imagine the PRS has no time to study every arrangement notified to it and consequently the most well-known traditional songs tend automatically to receive low gradings, and it's up to the publisher to send in a manuscript of a really original arrangement so that, having read it, the committee can see that it deserves a higher grade. If all that is left of the original song in your arrangement is the general idea plus the title, you would frankly do better to change the title. There is no copyright in mere ideas so by changing the title you will end up with a completely original song which will not need to be downgraded. Although the PRS in the UK will register an arrangement without having seen it, this is not the case in many countries and if you make arrangements of traditional songs then be prepared for your publisher to ask you to make manuscript copies if you haven't already done so, for him to pass on to his sub-publishers in other countries, or they will be unable to notify the arrangements, and you will receive no fees from performances in those countries.

How many old songs are actually traditional?

Quite a large number of songs including the likes of 'Greensleeves', 'Camptown Races' etc., are widely known to be traditional, but our advice is to check up if you are at all uncertain about the copyright status of a piece of music. If a man wrote songs at the age of thirty and died at the age of eighty the songs will be a hundred years old before they enter the so-called 'public domain' and become traditional in the UK.

This inevitably includes an enormous number of old Victorian songs which most people would assume must be out of copyright. The children's songs "Happy Birthday To You" and "I Know An Old Lady Who Swallowed A Fly" are both still copyright and will remain so for several decades! Victorian Music Hall songs like "Down At The Old Bull And Bush" and "Any Old Iron" are almost all still copyright (though "I Do Like To Be Beside The Seaside" no longer is). Some composers — or rather arrangers — have made considerable sums in recent times by virtue of 'arrangements' of other traditional songs: e.g.

"Amazing Grace" and "The Entertainer". In the case of "The Entertainer" it was vital that the new arranger/publisher omitted 'Theme from the film "The Sting" ' or called it "The Sting" as you would be implying that yours was the exact arrangement used in the film which of course is someone else's copyright. If you are going to 'borrow' a non-copyright song then make absolutely sure that you extract passages from the original and not the latest version which may well include original and new material and if you accidentally used any of that then you would be infringing copyright. The music and/or the words may have been changed. So be warned! You may reasonably believe that Christmas Carols are all out of copyright. But some are and some aren't. The "Twelve Days Of Christmas" is traditional in its original form but if you were to copy in your arrangement the rather distinctive and most used version which makes a musical change with 'five golden rings' then you would be in a copyright problem, for that line was originally written to be performed in exactly the same way as the other lines and only more recently did somebody change it. Most old folk songs and negro spirituals are traditional, but with these there may be other problems. UK copyright law per-

mits people to claim copyright in 'collected' songs on the grounds that the general public knew nothing of the songs until these people discovered them and collected them together in books, the most notable of such people being a gentleman named Cecil Sharp. It is thanks to him that children now sing songs like "Dashing Away With The Smoothing Iron", but it is because of him that you could not now make your own new arrangement of it. In the case of old American work songs and spirituals, enterprising people such as Alan

Lomax have devoted their lives to the discovery of their singers in rural America, and any arrangement which you might make of one of these old songs may well turn out to be based not on the original but on a previous, copyrighted arrangement by the singer.

How can I find out whether a song is traditional?

The 'Repertoire' department of the PRS will answer queries on whether a song or piece of music is copyright. You can write in to them (address is in the list of 'useful addresses' at the end) but remember that they are extremely busy, so try not to query more than a title or two at a time, and try to give them the composer's name if you can find it. This is a help to them as they have many different songs by different composers but all with the same title, including almost 500 different songs all called "I Love You"! If you are intending to give your arrangements to a publisher he will advise you as to whether or not the songs really are traditional.

Can I make arrangements of songs which are recent?

If you wish for any reason to perform or record a song which you know very well to be a recent work whose writer is still alive, it is most unlikely he or his publisher will try to stop you, but nevertheless you cannot claim to own it or take the arrangement to another publisher and ask him to do anything with it, as all the royalties which are earned by your version, no matter how original, will be paid to the original writer and his publisher, and you will not receive any part of them.

Are there any subjects to avoid in song lyrics?

Ten or twenty years ago this was a highly awkward subject. Records could be withdrawn or banned by the BBC for seemingly the most trivial reasons. In the present permissive age there is far less to worry about, but it is still advisable not to go too far on certain subjects, these being, use of brand names, sex, wanton violence, sheer distastefullness (so-called sick songs), religion, royalty and public figures plus, of course, anything libellous. Other countries sometimes have stricter standards than the UK. Ray Davies of the

Kinks was forced at the last minute, due to a ban in the US, to change 'Coca-Cola' in the song "Lola" into 'Cherry-Cola' and the same situation has happened to the Rolling Stones over "Let's Spend The Night Together" which had to become "Let's Spend Some

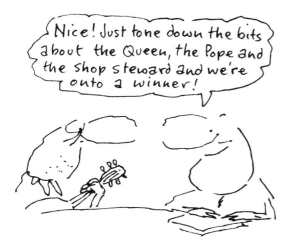

Time Together" for the USA. The BBC now adopts the view over brand names that if they are words like 'Rolls-Royce' or 'Cadillac' which are instantly recognisable and are really the best words for the job in the lyric, then this is permissible. Otherwise not.

Is there any formal body looking after the interests of songwriters?

Yes. These exist in many countries. The society in the UK for pop and light music writers is called the British Academy of Songwriters, Composers and Authors.

There is a yearly subscription to this society which produces standard publishing contracts for the use of its members and will give advice generally on songwriting and the music business. It also produces a regular newsletter for its members. This is also the body which has for many years, formerly under its old name of the Songwriters' Guild, presented the Ivor Novello

Awards annually to the best or most successful British song, writer, or piece of music in various categories.

Is there a body which can advise me on the status of individual publishers?

Whilst it isn't really for anyone to say whether one publisher is better than another, there is a body called the 'Music Publishers' Association' and it would be reasonable to presume that a member of the MPA will be reputable and will be properly in the publishing business. Needless to say if you know someone who has been in the business for a while he will be the obvious person to approach with questions such as these.

Can I use as many pen-names as I like?

There is nothing to stop you, particularly on songs which are printed in books but which you are not expecting ever to be broadcast or recorded. The PRS does ask however that you use not more than two different pen-names as it can become highly confusing.

Can I write a song with the same title as an existing song?

Broadly speaking the answer is yes, as there is no copyright in titles. Nevertheless you would probably lose out if you wrote songs with the same titles as big standards, as any money which your songs earned might be credited in error to the owners of the well-known songs. It is also best to steer clear of very distinctive and long titles like "Tie A Yellow Ribbon Round The Old Oak Tree" as anyone else seeing that title might be annoyed to find that it wasn't the well-known song, and the publisher would doubtless be incensed. The PRS will tell you, if you write to them, whether a certain title has been used before, but if you haven't heard of it it's probably OK for you to use it too.

RECORDING

GETTING A RECORD CONTRACT

Perhaps more than anything else for a singer or musician hoping to be a star, the idea of getting a recording contract is his great ambition, and in the eyes of his friends and relatives once he has been offered a contract he will already have "made it". Unfortunately this may be a very long way from the truth, if the contract is a bad one.

Which company should I approach?

When deciding which record company to approach first, it is naturally logical to pick one which is successful with your type of music. If for instance you are a 'reggae' artist, take a look at the reggae records which you or your friends may already have and approach these companies first. The only time when this might not be advisable is if you model yourself on one particular distinctive artist. A company is unlikely to be interested in signing you up if it already has an artist just like you, and in any case this would not be in your interest, because the bigger artist would have the pick of all the suitable songs which had been submitted to the company by publishers.

How can I make the best impression?

In the final analysis, unless a talent scout from a particular record company comes look-

ing for you, you will just have to hawk your demonstration tapes (or yourself) round until someone expresses interest in you. If the first few companies don't, remember you've lost nothing, and don't despair. Many famous artists, including the Beatles, have been turned down by very knowledgeable and successful people in the music business before finally being signed up.

An alternative to visiting a record company, particularly if you don't have any tapes of yourself or your group, is to convince somebody from the company over the telephone that you are well worth hearing and suggest that they come to hear you at your next booking, provided that the management don't object, and provided that you're pretty sure it will be a good performance and you will have a favourable reception.

If you do want to take some tapes along to a record company for them to hear, it's obviously best if you can avoid having to play tapes recorded in your sitting room. People frequently submit tapes made at home to record companies. They can be adequate if they are recorded on a good tape recorder and only feature voice and guitar. A record company man with an experienced ear will be able to penetrate the warp and crackle to decide whether the artist on the tape has any talent. This being the case, incidentally, do bear in mind that if your tape is constantly rejected by record companies it will probably not be because they are unimpressed by the poor tape quality, but because they are un-impressed by the performance on the tape, or maybe by the songs being played. It might be better if you're convinced that you're good enough to make the grade, not to try every company but to go back and practice or just make a new tape and try it on some different companies. If you play your first tape to all of the major companies and not one of them likes your first effort you'll be less likely to succeed with your second tape than with your first, as the people listening will be expecting something mediocre and it will take something pretty dynamic to get over this inbuilt prejudice. If you leave it for say a year before

you try a second time, however, you may find that the people listening are entirely different from those who heard your first tape (faces change quickly in the music business) and you'll again have the advantage of being an unknown quantity.

Returning to the subject of your tapes, it is obviously true that a poor tape doesn't create a very good impression, especially if the tape is of a group, and if you are prepared to invest a bit of money in your musical career, you can make your own recording in a studio.

How can I make a demonstration record?

Studios are not all the exclusive property of record companies. Most of them are independent, and smaller ones can be hired privately for as little as around £10 per hour, plus cost of tape and incidental expenses. A competent group, who don't keep making odd little mistakes, should be able to put down at least three songs during a three hour session, or even more if they're not quite so concerned with the quality of the resulting tapes. If you can do it during an ordinary working day (so that the engineer at the studio doesn't have to be paid overtime etc.) the total cost can be as low as £40. The all-important first impression with the record companies who hear the tapes will be very much more favourable. The better (and generally the more

expensive) the studio, the better your demos will probably be.

The above is all very fine for groups. A straight singer who normally sings to a combo or orchestral backing could hire or cajole a pianist to accompany him, but the hiring of professional musicians is very expensive and is not worthwhile at this stage if costs are to be kept low.

Some studios have equipment giving as much as sixty-four tracks — enough for each member of an orchestra's performance to be recorded separately before being blended with the others. The most you will really need for a 'demo' tape will be four tracks, one for drums, one for bass, one for vocals and one for guitar or piano, for instance. Some studios charge different rates for the number of tracks you want e.g. £15 for 4-track, £20 for 8-track per hour. Most studios can cut 'acetates' or 7-inch demonstration discs from tapes. These cost something over £1.50 for a single-sided disc as a guideline. It is rather impressive, apparently to have a 'record' of yourself, but

the quality will not be quite as good as the tape, and it will deteriorate noticeably after a number of plays.

UK RECORDING STUDIOS

The following is a list of studios covering many parts of the country. Obviously not every small studio is listed here, and some which are included will be outside the range of your pocket or your requirements, but they will always quote their rates to you on request. Purely by virtue of their importance and size some of the larger studios are not listed. If you are wondering which particular studios to contact, you would be well advised to seek the help of an organisation called the Association of Professional Recording Studios Ltd., 23 Chestnut Avenue, Chorleywood, Herts. (Chorleywood 72907). They have their own list of recording studios and will be willing to advise you.

Amazon Studios,
Music House,
ISD Stopgate Lane,
Simonswood,
Liverpool,
Merseyside.

Ark Recording Studios,
2 Fairfield Road,
Kingston-upon-Thames,
Surrey.

Audiogenic Studio,
34-36 Crown Street,
Reading,
Berks.

Beck Recording Studios,
Lister Road,
Wellingborough,
Northants.

BGS Productions,
Kirtlend Park Studios,
Lethane Road,
Strathaven,
Scotland.

Bridge Studios,
77 Weiss Road,
Putney,
London SW15.

Cargo Recording Studios,
Kenion Street,
Rochdale,
Lancs.

Ca Va Sound Studio,
49 Derby Street,
Kelvingrove,
Glasgow,
Scotland.

Chipping Norton Recording
Studios Ltd.,
28-30 New Street,
Chipping Norton,
Oxon.

Craighall Recording Studio,
68 Craighall Road,
Edinburgh EH6 4RL,
Scotland.

Druids Studios,
40 Sawsbury Road,
Dagenham,
Essex.

East Anglian Productions,
21-23 Walton Road,
Frinton-on-Sea,
Essex.

Eden Studios,
20-24 Beaumont Road,
Chiswick,
London W4.

Essar Music,
The Coach House,
High Street,
Farningham,
Kent.

Fairview Music,
Great Gutter Lane,
Willerby,
Hull,
Humberside.

Fanfare Records,
1 Broomfield Close,
Rydes Hill,
Guildford,
Surrey.

Folktracks,
2 Fircliff Park,
Portishead,
Bristol,
Avon.

Frog Studios,
4 Ashcombe Gardens,
Edgware,
Middlesex.

Galaxy Music Productions,
62a West Street,
Harwich,
Essex.

Hollywood Studios,
38-40 Upper Clapton Road,
London E5.

Impulse Sound Studio,
71 High Street E.,
Wallsend,
Tyne & Wear.

Jigsaw Studios,
115 Old Lodge Lane,
Purley,
Surrey.

Leader Sound Studios,
209 Rochdale Road,
Greetland,
Halifax,
Yorks.

Livingston Studios,
Brook Road,
London N22.

Lower Whopping Conker Company,
45 Victoria Road,
Romford,
Essex.

Lysander Studios,
Unit 4,
Lysander Road,
Bowerhill,
Melksham,
Wiltshire.

Manor Studios,
Shipton-on-Cherwell,
Kidlington,
Oxford,
Oxon.

Mountain Rehearsal Studios,
Pant y Cerrig,
Llanfynydd,
Dyfed,
Wales.

Multicord,
3 Ravensworth View,
Dunston,
Tyne & Wear.

Mushroom Studios 52,
18 West Mall,
Clifton,
Bristol,
Avon.

Oakwood Studios,
75 Strode Park Road,
Herne Bay,
Kent.

Off Beat Studio,
4 Aberdeen Grove,
Armley,
Leeds 12,
W. Yorkshire.

Old Smithy Recording Studio,
1 Post Office Lane,
Kempsey,
Worcs.

Orwell-Endwell Music,
127 Aldersgate Street,
London EC1.

Outlet Homespun Recording Co.,
48 Smithfield Square,
West Belfast,
N. Ireland.

Oz Studios,
48 Tamworth Lane,
Mitcham,
Surrey.

Pan-Audio Ltd.,
4 Forth Street,
Edinburgh EH1 3LD,
Scotland.

Pandora Music,
25 Chapel Street,
Wellesbourne,
Stratford-upon-avon,
Warwickshire.

Parkgates Studio,
Parkgate Cottage,
Catsfield,
Battle,
Sussex.

Playfar,
10 Landsdowne Gardens,
Hailsham,
East Sussex.

Pluto Recording Studio,
36 Granby Road,
Manchester 1,
Lancashire.

Q Studios,
1487 Melton Road,
Queniborough,
Leicester,
Leics.

Quest Studios,
71 Windmill Road,
Luton,
Bedfordshire.

Ramport Studios,
115-117 Thessaly Road,
Battersea,
London SW8.

Red Shop Recorders,
236 St. Paul's Road,
Islington,
London N1.

Revolution Studios,
11 Church Road,
Cheadle Hume,
Cheshire.

Roche Recording Studio,
Tremodrett,
Roche,
Cornwall.

Schoolhouse Recording Studio,
The Old Schoolhouse,
Whitecairns,
Aberdeen,
Scotland.

Sin City Studios,
22a Forest Road West,
Nottingham,
Notts.

M. Stevens & Partners,
216-218 Homesdale Road,
Bromley,
Kent.

Strawberry Recording Studios
(UK),
3 Waterloo Road,
Stockport,
Cheshire.

Surrey Sound Studios,
70 Kingston Road,
Leatherhead,
Surrey.

Tabitha Studios,
39 Cordery Road,
Exeter,
Devon.

Temple Records Studio,
Shillinghill,
Temple Midlothian,
Scotland.

Trend Studios,
70 Hagan Court,
Lad Lane,
Lower Baggot Street,
Dublin 2,
Eire.

Waterloo Studios,
Gorsey Mount Street,
Stockport,
Cheshire.

Wickham Recording Studios,
121 Canterbury Road,
Croydon,
Surrey.

Zella Recording Studios,
Walker Hall,
Ampton Road,
Edgbaston,
Birmingham,
W. Midlands.

UK RECORD COMPANIES

The most important factor in selling your recording services to a record company is of course to know who and where the record companies are. For this reason we have included here a list of addresses of British record companies. Don't think that just because a company is not on this list it's automatically not worth signing with. New companies are being formed all the time (regrettably many go out of business after just a few releases) and it is not possible to produce a fully comprehensive list. It is always a good idea to refer also to current Yellow Pages, Local Directories and the latest Trade publications (like the 'Music & Video Week' Directory). It would be wrong to assume that all the companies on this list, or in any other publication, are crying out for new acts all the time. They may have more than they can cope with at a certain time, or you may not really be what they're looking for even if they admit that you're good. Nevertheless few people will turn down something which they really think is sensational.

Remember that many of these companies have several different record labels under which they release their records. If you look at one of these labels you will sometimes find the name of the parent company on it. It is as well to remember, if you are looking for a major company to whom to offer your services, that a large proportion of the charts each week is made up of American records, and some of the companies who regularly have hits with these are concerned comparatively little with British artists.

Notable omissions from this list are companies such as K-Tel, Ronco, Arcade, Readers' Digest, etc. The reason for this is that such companies are principally concerned with compilations of other record companies' products, although they may make some productions themselves.

A & M Records,
136-140 New Kings Road,
London SW6.

Ariola/Arista Records,
3 Cavendish Square,
London W1.

BBC Records & Tapes,
The Langham,
Portland Place,
London W1.

Bronze Records,
100 Chalk Farm Road,
London NW1.

Carrere Records,
22 Queen Street,
Mayfair,
London W1.

CBS Records,
17-19 Soho Square,
London W1.

Charisma Records,
90 Wardour Street,
London W1.

Cherry Red Records,
53 Kensington Gardens Square,
London W2.

Chrysalis Records,
12 Stratford Place,
London W1.

Creole Records,
91-93 High Street,
Harlesden,
London NW10.

Decca Records,
50 New Bond Street,
London W1.

DJM Records,
James House,
5-11 Theobalds Road,
London WC1.

EG Records,
63a Kings Road,
London SW3.

Emerald Records,
120 Coach Road,
Templepatrick,
Ballyclare,
Co. Antrim,
N. Ireland.

EMI Records,
EMI House,
20 Manchester Square,
London W1.

Ensign Records,
3 Monmouth Place,
London W2.

ERC Records,
46 South Molton Street,
London W1.

Factory Records,
86 Palatine Road,
Didsbury,
Manchester 20.

Hansa Productions,
26 Castlereach Street,
London W1.

Island Records,
22 St. Peter's Square,
London W6.

Jive Records,
165 Willesden High Road,
London NW10.

Logo Records,
52 Red Lion Street,
London WC1.

Magnet records,
Magnet House,
22 York Street,
London W1.

MAM Records,
24-25 New Bond Street,
London W1.

MCA Records,
1 Great Pulteney Street,
London W1.

Motown Int.,
16 Curzon Street,
London W1.

Mute Records,
49-53 Kensington Gardens
Square,
London W2.

Phonogram Records,
50 New Bond Street,
London W1.

Pinnacle Records,
1 Oasthouse Way,
Cray Avenue,
Orpington,
Kent.

Polydor,
13-14 St. George Street,
London W1.

President Records,
Broadmead House,
21 Panton Street,
London SW1.

PRT,
ACC House,
17 Great Cumberland Place,
London W1.

RAK Records,
42-48 Charlbert Street,
London NW8.

RCA Records,
1 Bedford Avenue,
London WC1.

Riva Records,
2 New Kings road,
London SW6.

Rocket Records,
125 Kensington High Street,
London W8.

Rough Trade Records,
137 Blenheim Crescent,
London W1..

RSO Records & Tapes,
67 Brook Street,
London W1.

Safari Records,
44 Seymour Place,
London W1.

Satril Records,
444 Finchley Road,
London NW2.

Sonet Records & Publishing,
121 Ledbury Road,
London W1.

Spartan Records,
London Road,
Wembley,
Middlesex.

State Records,
26-27 Castlereagh Street,
London W1.

Stiff Records,
115-123 Bayham Street,
London NW1.

Trojan Records,
104 High Street,
Harlesden,
London NW10.

Valentine Music Group,
7 Garrick Street,
London WC2.

Virgin Records,
2-4 Vernon Yard,
119 Portobello Road,
London W11.

WEA Records,
20 Broadwick Street,
London W1.

Zomba Productions,
165-167 Willesden High Road,
London NW10.

RECORD COMPANIES

In the last few years literally hundreds of new record companies have mushroomed in the world's major music centres. Many of these are owned by managers, producers, publishers or artists themselves hoping partly to become independent of the fairly small number of major companies who have for decades dominated the market in most countries and partly to cash in on the very large profits which can be made by issuing purely successful records. They often fail to appreciate the very heavy costs involved in recording, pressing, distribution and advertising frequently wasted on records which only sell a few hundred copies.

Will they always want to give me a blanket contract?

With songwriting, you are not always asked to sign an exclusive long-term contract, but with recording this is almost always the case. A record company will not normally chance making and releasing one record to 'see what happens' without having options to keep you for a long term if you turn out to be a sensation. This is understandable as recording is expensive and a quite straightforward single can easily cost from £500 to produce plus the cost of manufacture and advertising. So you will be offered a contract, generally for one or two years, under the terms of which the company will, or should be required to record you a minimum number of times per contract year (but remember this does not necessarily mean they have actually to release the recordings). They'll also have options to extend the contract up to an overall period of three or five years generally on slightly better terms each time. If your records sell badly, then most record companies will be only too pleased to call it a day at the end of the first term. If you are successful then resign yourself to being with that company for the longest possible term under the contract. You may be perfectly happy with them. Sometimes contracts are even changed in your favour during the period of the contract. Some record companies however stick rigidly to what might be the minimum royalty terms of the contract even though you have become an important part of their roster, not realising apparently that they are making you determined to clear off at the first chance you get. Probably the worst thing to happen is to be almost a success i.e. your records have sold well enough for the record company to recover its costs and show a small profit. Consequently they've lost nothing, but you may have spent the best years of your career for next to

nothing, and 'Joe Public' will still say 'who?', when your name is mentioned. One hit however, and of course other doors open, and the £100 gig rockets to £1,000 and more per appearance almost overnight. How much of that you will see is another matter (see 'Artist Management' section).

One provision which is well worth asking for in a recording contract is that the contract terminates after say one year unless a recording produced during that year featuring you has been included in the top 30 or 50 of a recognised British (or overseas) chart, preferably as played by the BBC. If your record has made the charts then probably you will both wish the company to renew the contract for further periods. If it hasn't made the charts then you are simply free to go elsewhere at the end of that first year.

What royalties will I get under a recording contract?

The amount will be shown as a percentage and is usually based (as with song royalties) on the retail price of the record, less VAT, but sometimes the contract refers to the wholesale selling price or somesuch, and with the customary trade discounts thrown in, it is often very hard to work out what you can really expect to receive. Is 10% wholesale better than 6% retail? Strangely the answer is probably no! So our advice is to ask what you can expect to get in pence (but *never* have the royalty expressed in pence for although 10p a copy may be all right when the retail price of a single is £1.50 if the price increases your royalty won't!). A new artist may start with a royalty (which based on a £1.50 single) will give him around 9p per single, increasing to 14p at the end of the contract. Note that if you have a hit at the end of the contract with a record you made at the beginning you'll invariably be paid at the rate which applied when the recording was made. The rates for foreign sales are usually half the UK rate (Eire counts as UK).

Will I be paid for every record sold?

Usually you will only be paid on 90% of actual sales, sometimes less. This is to cover returns, breakages and faulty records etc. Suppose you know that your record has sold 100,000 (incidentally beware of sales figures shown in the music press, as publicity people tend to exaggerate and a chart entry does not always mean good sales but could be a fiddle or mistake — they do happen). And suppose your royalty works out at 3p per record, then don't expect to get £3,000. Why? Firstly the 100,000 gross becomes 90,000 (or less) net (i.e. £2,700) and after deduction of recording costs you may well end up with more like £2,000. On LP's and tapes etc., there will also be discounts in respect of 'container charges' (LP sleeves, cartridges etc.) and in the case of 'budget' LP's your royalty will almost certainly be halved. As budget LP's are normally cheap in any case and therefore the normal royalty would in any case be low this seems surprising perhaps. Nevertheless this has become accepted practice and is quite normal.

Who pays the recording costs?

It is important to find out whether the record company intends to recover its recording costs before paying you any royalties. This is obviously not good for you but is pretty normal. Worse than this, and in very many cases, they may recover the costs entirely out of royalties which they would have paid to you, which obviously means your record has to sell far far more before they start paying you. Although by doing this they effectively make you pay for the recording, it does not mean that you own it. Worst of all they may add together the costs of all your recordings and deduct the whole lot before paying you, which of course means you can have a No. 1 hit single but because you've just had a flop LP you won't get a penny.

Will the company pay my travelling expenses?

The answer is not usually, and it could be very expensive for a group who live in Scotland recording an LP in London over a period of days or weeks. Some companies may give

you an advance against your royalties to help you out, although in effect this still means that you end up paying. Some will simply pay your reasonable expenses out of their own pockets as it were. They'll also usually be as helpful as possible in finding a date and time which are convenient to you although the contract will state that provided the company gives you reasonable notice that they want you, then you must be there.

Some contracts state that if you fail to turn up for no good reason then you have to pay, or have deducted from your royalties, the entire cost of the session booked, including cancellation fees to the studio, backing musicians, orchestras etc. If you have a perfectly good excuse for your absence then this

could be grossly unfair on you. If on the other hand you continually fail to appear at sessions which you have previously agreed were perfectly convenient for you then of course you are being grossly unfair to the record company, who will probably lose patience and drop you unless you are a superstar, in which case they will excuse you on the grounds of 'artistic temperament'!

When will I be paid?

Royalties should be paid twice yearly to your last known address (so whatever you do make sure you tell them if you move). The contract may say that they'll pay you 'as soon as possible' after 30th June and 31st December, which really is too vague. Try to make sure that it says 'within X days after . . .' (sixty should be perfectly reasonable, although it may sound a long time). Make sure that the record company will continue to pay you on records made by you which are sold after the contract has finished and you are no longer recording for that company. You'd think this would be obvious, but one international record company has issued contracts stating that the royalties cease at the end of the contract, even though they can go on selling the artist's records!

Can they stop paying me for any reason?

Another major company's contract allows them to withhold your royalties if you lose your voice or talent or if you die before the contract has finished. As these reasons are beyond your control this is totally unfair to you (or next of kin) as is the withholding of royalties if you are unable, through no fault of yours to turn up for sessions as we mentioned earlier.

What happens about photographs and publicity?

Under the contract you give the company the right to use your name, biography, photographs etc. for publicity purposes. This is quite reasonable and necessary for the company but make sure that they don't expect you to pay, or have deducted from your royalties, costs of photographic sessions etc. which they themselves have arranged for you. The photographs will be for their purposes. Under the contract they will be entitled to use

whatever photographs of you they choose (or none at all) on LP sleeves, posters, press advertisements etc.

What about LP's with different artists on each track?

Although rare in the past 'compilation albums', as they are called, are now an established feature of the record scene and practically every record company issues mixed LP's of good items from their catalogues (or licenses people like K-Tel to do so). This shouldn't worry you and you won't lose by it, for generally these productions are good sellers and extra mileage is obtained from what was otherwise a long gone hit of yours. If you normally get 5% artist royalty for your LP's and your recording is one of say twelve different tracks on a 'compilation album' then you will get one-twelfth of 5% of the total retail selling price (less tax) of the LP. Incidentally LP's are often called 'albums' in the music business. This is an American term and is sometimes confusing because in the UK 'albums' has also tended to mean song books. So if someone starts talking to you about 'albums' make sure that you know what they mean.

What happens if I am part of a duo or group?

If you are performing and recording with others then, invariably, you will all be asked to sign with the company although sometimes there is only one member in which the recording company is really interested and if that's you then you will have to do some heart-searching and decide whether you really want to succeed without your friends. On the assumption however that the duo or group or whatever is wanted by the company then they will either offer you separate but identical contracts or one collective agreement. Either way you will end up sharing the total royalty. The individual contract may well say that the artist royalty is, in effect, '5% retail' or somesuch but it will then go on to say that the royalty is reduced pro rata with other artists performing on the recording who are entitled to receive royalties. The 'other artists' of course will be the rest of the group who each have identical agreements. Although this wording will also cover the record company in the event of them wanting you to record with another of their contract artists, what this very definitely

That's not me?!

SCROTTY BOYLES!

shouldn't mean however is that your royalties are reduced pro rata with any session musicians playing on your records.

What happens if the group splits up?

If you leave the group and are replaced then a record company will probably not be interested in you and will not take up their next option on your contract. You may well find however that the record company will continue to regard you as a contract artist. Even if you join a group under contract to some other company, should you start recording again for that company during what would have been the period of the first contract then the first record company may well take legal action against you and/or the new company. So if you leave a group make sure that everyone who has a hand in your career knows of your intentions and that you obtain a letter of release from one company before recording for another.

Is it right that some groups don't play on their own records?

Not only is it right, but it's still quite common with a new group who are not used to recording. Studio time is so expensive that they sometimes use seasoned professionals for everything except the voice to start with. They just can't afford to have anyone there who might fluff a note. If this does happen to you, don't worry about your royalties – you will get your share of whatever is due under the contract regardless.

Will I have any say in LP designs or notes?

Probably not, but if you have any very good or positive ideas then a progressive company will usually take them into consideration, although don't be disappointed if they don't because the sleeve is a major selling factor with many LP's, and the company must be regarded as knowing best on these matters.

Should songwriting and merchandising be mentioned in the contract?

There should be no mention in the contract of your songwriting services. Some companies try to pick these up in the record contract as though it were quite normal. In fact it's

nothing of the kind, and if you were already signed to a publisher as a blanket writer and you then signed a record contract with this in it you'd end up in the middle of legal wrangle! Some companies' contracts allow them to market goods other than records and tapes which have become closely associated with you. If they grant a firm permission to make and sell distinctive 'Joe Smith' T-Shirts, posters, badges or other merchandise they'll probably pay you a mere fraction of what your

manager could get for you if he approached the manufacturer direct.

Who decides what songs I should record?

Generally the record company, especially with 'middle of the road' artists, sales of whose LP's can be drastically reduced by the inclusion of even a few original or unknown tracks. Otherwise most companies will maybe let you have your own way with a track or two on an LP or the B-side of a single (especially if their publishing affiliate owns the publishing rights to your songs) and if you're a songwriter/singer then the material will probably all be original anyway (though they'll still want to choose what they think are the best tracks). If they want you to record a song which you recorded only a few years back for another company then check to make sure that your agreement with that other company didn't prevent you, or you could be in trouble. The copyright people at your company will happily look over the old agreement for you if you ask them to check such things as this.

Can they hold me to the contract if I'm under 18?

Under the age of eighteen you are legally a minor. If you were under eighteen when you signed, and the contract was in any way thrust upon you, then the chances are that you can revoke it by threatening legal action or getting a solicitor to do this, unless the company can prove that it has showered you with money and publicity. On the other hand if your parent or guardian counter-signed the contract which you signed, and if it was all clearly explained to you and you apparently understood it then you can probably be held to it regardless of your age.

How would I get out of a recording contract?

Ultimately of course a record company can't make you go into a studio and record. If you've hardly earned anything from your records, and don't expect to, then you won't be bothered with any threat to withhold your royalties. However, the best way out of a recording contract, as with a publishing contract, is by mutual agreement, although you should expect to be asked to pay back any advance payment that the record company has given you which they haven't yet recovered from your royalties. If this fails then there are three possibilities. Firstly, they may not have taken up one of their options to extend the contract. This may mean waiting till a certain date and hoping that the letter of extension doesn't arrive. If it doesn't then write to them straightaway telling them politely that you note that they haven't taken up their option to renew and in view of this you intend to place your services elsewhere. If you carry on recording for them for some time after the renewal date however even though the contract was not properly renewed, then your position becomes less strong. Secondly, they may have failed repeatedly to send royalty statements to you at the times set out in the contract (usually twice a year). If the contract says that they are not obliged to send a statement when there is little or no money due to you then this is probably the reason if you have had no statements for a while. Otherwise the statements should have arrived even if no money was due. If it has been over

a year since you last received a statement write pointing this out and asking for one. After a few weeks write again (politely, not threateningly), and if you again receive no reply you should consult a solicitor who will tell you whether in the particular circumstances you have been sufficiently reasonable and the company sufficiently unreasonable for you to rescind (i.e. simply declare yourself free from) the contract. There is no harm in asking the solicitor what his charge is likely to be, although he won't of course be able to tell you very precisely until he knows exactly how you stand. If you have already written the polite letters and if you are sure that there is money owing to you then it will be well worth while to consult the solicitor. If you are wanted by another record company, they may put their solicitor onto the case and pay his fees themselves. Thirdly, it may be that the record company has failed to record the agreed number of tracks with you during the current term of the agreement to enable them to renew (obviously you will have to wait until the end of the current term before you can say this for certain). If they recorded say nine tracks in the first year and only two in the second, and their commitment under the contract was five tracks per year then they may or may not be covered, depending on the exact wording of the contract.

Will I be completely tied to the company?

Your services will be exclusive to the record company, so make sure you ask them first if you want to do even one session for another company (they'll very often go along with this provided they get a royalty and credit on the record). If a record company wishes to sign you up, but you're playing regularly on sessions elsewhere, you may be able to get them to sign you exclusively under your own name, but leave you free to work elsewhere unnamed or under pseudonyms (there's no limit to the number of these you can have as an artist). They'll require you not to re-record for another company any song which you recorded for them for a number of years after the contract has finished. If this clause were not included then you could have a hit in the last month of your contract and go straight off to another company, re-record the same song and put it out in competition. Three to five years is a reasonable period but over five is certainly excessive and represents a restraint on your livelihood which may not be legally enforceable, so if you ignored it and re-recorded a song elsewhere five years later they probably couldn't stop you – check with a solicitor.

Should I sign with an independent record producer?

Independent producers are very often management/publishing concerns with surplus cash which they're prepared to invest in the making of records, either in their own or in hired-out studios. Unlike most of the record companies, good independent producers are not restricted to London or other major music centres. They lease the records to an actual record company in return for a royalty of say 8% – 14%, out of which they should pay you as an artist X% not of what they get, but of the retail selling price of the records (as if you were signed to the record company itself). They will want to sign you up for a total of several years just as a record company itself would, because the record company to whom they lease your record will want to be guaranteed further recordings. There is no reason at all why you should not sign with an independent producer if he's properly 'in business' though it may well be as well to ascertain that your records will come out on a recognised successful label.

Whereas an independent producer should guarantee to record a certain number of songs with you regularly, he cannot of course guarantee that they will be released. The usual way in which independent producers work is to make one single with a new artist and take it round the record companies in the hope that one of them will agree to release it. If they do then they will usually want your exclusive output for at least a year or two and the length of the deal which they make with the independent producer will determine the length of the deal he makes with you, or the number of options on you that the independent producer takes up. The record company itself may well ask you to sign a small agreement directly with it, whereby if you and your independent producer part company before the end of his deal with the record company then you have to record directly for the record company for the rest of the duration of that deal. If this small agreement states that you will sign the record company's standard artist agreement or somesuch phrase than ask to see it, as it may contain certain clauses whereby you end up with less than the royalty the independent producer was paying you! Thus if you become dissatisfied with your independent producer and parted company before the end of his contract with you you would still be bound by the small agreement to record for the commercial company and you might be jumping out of the frying pan into the fire. Again, read and understand, everything you are asked to sign.

Could I make my own records?

In recent years many independent producers, including many outside London, have taken to pressing their own records in small quantities and getting a major record company to distribute them. Some of these small labels have become very successful, usually with a specific type of music. Others are actually owned and run by a group or artist themselves, who have had some money behind them but were unable or unwilling to get a deal with an established record company. Only one step down from this is a one-off LP or single recorded and pressed by an amateur singer or group.

It is possible on a shoestring budget and using your own or a borrowed 2 or 4 track sound on sound tape recorder or cassette recorder (or a very cheap local studio) to make and arrange for the pressing of a single for as little as £1,000 or so, including printing of a basic picture sleeve and payment of copyright royalties by prior arrangement with the MCPS (mentioned elsewhere) on behalf of the publishers who control the songs you are recording (even if they are your own songs which you have assigned to a publisher). It is uneconomical to press less than 500-1,000 records. Although LP's are fairly expensive to press, store, sleeve and mail out, cassettes can even be duplicated at home as long as the quality is passable and copyright requirements are observed and royalties paid. The MCPS are most helpful to anyone wanting information about duplicating or pressing their own records or tapes and wanting to know how to comply with the law.

Some studios, if they are impressed by you, will forego part or all of their studio hire fees in return for an undertaking by you to pay them around 2% on the retail price of any records or tapes sold of the recordings you make in their studio, provided you are doing it on a commercial basis. This could be a way round an initial shortage of cash.

GENERAL QUESTIONS AND ANSWERS ON RECORDING

Will I get a royalty when my record is broadcast?

Yes. A fee is collected by an organisation called 'Phonographic Performance Ltd'. This is then paid to the record company, provided it's a member, and the artist separately. You don't have to claim the fees, join the organisation or anything, but if you are getting a lot of plays on the BBC you should be assured of these fees provided the record company has supplied PPL with your home address (which they should do, but don't always). If you're not getting the fees, chase up your record company about it. You must be a 'featured' artist to collect the fees, i.e. generally your name, or the name of a group of which you are a regular member, must appear on the record label, and you will be receiving a royalty not just a session fee.

If I'm offered a royalty or session fee which should I take?

If you are not signed exclusively to one record company, but are a musician playing on sessions for various companies, there may be occasions when you will be offered either a session fee or a royalty on a particular recording. Generally if you are a 'featured' artist (i.e. your name will appear on the record label) you should choose the royalty just in case the record becomes a hit. Hit records do still happen made by artists who were paid only the fee for the session (this sort of thing makes the National Press). Obviously if you really need the ready money and you don't think the record stands an earthly chance of selling, you'll have to decide the case on its merits.

Is it a good idea to give my writing and recording services to the same company?

Not always. Many composers feel, though sometimes unfairly, that the publishing arm of a record company, knowing that their recording of this song is to be released by its associate is not going to be in too much of a hurry to and in fact may never wholeheartedly push that song around other record companies, to obtain more recordings of it. If you should ever suspect your record company of being at all dishonest in its accountings to you as an artist, you may well get no assistance from the company's own publishing associate, whereas if your song is with an entirely separate publisher, that publisher will probably investigate any doubts and fears you may have, as this will be in his interest as well as yours.

What should I know about recording sessions?

You probably already know what goes on at a recording session even if you have never

actually taken part in one yourself. The two vital people at a session, besides the artists themselves, are the Producer and the Engineer. Basically the Producer is the one who decides what sound he wants the record to have, what each instrument and voice should sound like, whether anything needs to be re-recorded and at what point the recording has been satisfactorily completed. The engineer sits at the mixing desk in the control room and actually achieves the sounds which the producer wants. The two tasks overlap considerably. Many producers have at one time been engineers, and could in fact do the whole thing themselves if they were familiar with the sound equipment of the studio being used.

If the studio has enough 'tracks' (mentioned earlier under 'making a demonstration record') then each instrument will be recorded separately. You will often have to play through each song several times for the Engineer to obtain the right sound before he even attempts to tape it, which is why proficient musicians are essential. If you are a singer recording any song you should make sure beforehand that you are given a copy of the song, firstly to familiarise yourself with it and secondly to look at during the session. Professional session musicians will expect to be given a copy of the music specially arranged for their instruments and will simply read this off, although members of a group should have 'routined' the song sufficiently beforehand that there is no question of them forgetting it if they cannot read music or have no music.

A session usually lasts about three hours during which time up to three songs may be recorded (three are normally recorded for a single release, so that the best two can be chosen). It may however be that the backing is recorded at one session and the vocals added at an entirely different time. Professional session musicians will be expected to arrive with their instruments, but a group should ask beforehand whether their instruments and equipment will be wanted on the session or whether the Producer and Engineer think it necessary to hire better equipment.

What should I be paid if I'm asked to produce a record?

It may well be that before too long you will find that you yourself know what sound you want your records to have and your record company will be quite satisfied with this. In this case you will not always need to have a producer present when you record and you may be given the credit for the production on labels or on LP sleeves. In this case a producer royalty of 2% on UK record sales and 1% overseas is acceptable. This may be more than doubled if you are producing hit records. This will of course be in addition to your artist royalty where your own records are concerned. If you are asked to produce records of other artists again 2% halved for foreign sales, is quite reasonable, although obviously if you make a name for yourself then you will be able to

command more. In all these instances you will probably find that the record company will not pay the royalty until they have recovered the costs of the production of the record. Naturally this is a very good incentive to you as the producer to keep the costs as low as possible. Some freelance producers can earn large sums by way of fees plus royalties on records they produce, and there are even companies acting as agencies for producers, finding them work and negotiating fees. Many record companies agree to pay artists a large advance against royalties per LP. Out of this must come the cost of recording the LP, but frequently the artists are at liberty to hire whichever studio they prefer, and if they are unhappy with their resident engineers or producers they will hire an independent one with whom they have worked before or who they think will do a good job for them. The fees and royalties payable to the independent producer will come out of the advance and royalty paid by the record company to the artists.

What do I get if I'm in a stage show which is recorded?

You will appreciate that a record company will not want to place the entire cast under contract. They probably would not be able to anyway, for many recording artists supplement their income by appearing in stage shows even though they may otherwise be under contract to another record company from the one which intends to record the show. What generally happens is that each member of the cast receives a session fee for the recording and separately the record company pays an Artist Royalty of at least 5% to the Actors Union, Equity.

ARTIST
MANAGEMENT

MANAGEMENT CONTRACTS

Public entertainers of all types have long been reliant for guidance in their careers upon professional managers. There comes a time in most semi-professional singers' and musicians' careers when they are simply too busy to worry about the business side of things, or when they feel that they are not busy enough and would like somebody to be hustling on their behalf, securing engagements, recording contracts and so forth.

Do I need a manager anyway?

This entirely depends upon just how busy you are as a performer and upon how much money you are making. It is possible to exist as a semi-professional or even a professional singer or musician for years without a manager, but once real success comes your way then you will probably need a manager. In the meantime you can get by with an agent to secure engagements for you at around 10% to 15% of the fee, plus an accountant to ensure that you pay as little tax as possible and maybe a solicitor occasionally to write the odd letter to any agency or venue which failed to pay you — if the uncollected fee is likely to be greater than the solicitor's charge, of course.

You can employ your own publicist, and secure recording and publishing contracts yourself (the relevant sections of this book explain what to do and what to sign). Nevertheless a manager worth his salt should be able to secure better royalty rates and terms than you could on your own. There are a great many songwriters with no aspirations towards being recording or performing artists, and writers usually negotiate with publishers themselves as they would have no other immediate need of a manager. Recording artists on the other hand are usually primarily performers and thus their managers who look after the 'live performance' side of their career usually deal on their behalf with record companies. (This is why the songwriting section of this book is somewhat longer than the recording section.) Bear in mind that some managers who are wizards at securing you good live engagements for high fees may know little about recording contracts, for which reason you should always ask to take away and look at a recording contract (or a publishing contract) which your manager has secured for you, in the light of this book.

Ultimately if you are a really successful artist you will also be really hardworking too, and will probably have to leave the running of business and everyday affairs to a manager.

How much control of my career will he want?

You should thrash this out with him very precisely before signing anything so that it is clearly understood what you both want. In a sense he is 'employing' you and at the same time you are 'employing' him. For this reason, although he will probably have agreements already with other artists and therefore have a sort of 'standard' contract, he may ask you to have the contract prepared yourself (for your guidance a form of management contract is enclosed with notes showing which clauses are reasonable for you and which are not, although you would certainly have to employ a solicitor, to produce a contract for you or simply to double-check the contract which you are offered).

You may be approached by a big-time management company who will ask you to sign a contract which puts you and your career completely in their hands for a number of years. On the other hand you may find a decent local chap with a few good contacts to 'manage' you. If your manager is determined that you'll only succeed if you change your image or buy a lot of new amplification equipment or a new wardrobe don't sign with him if you've no desire to do any of this to get to the top and are quite happy simply to be getting regular engagements. Remember that most managers will tell you and everyone else that you're great, and will be hoping, though maybe not expecting, to make a fortune out of you sooner or later, when you become the new Beatles, Elvis Presley, Led Zeppelin, Max Bygraves or whatever.

If you do have an agreement (even just a verbal one) with a local man whereby he gets a cut of your earnings, make sure that you terminate it, if it hasn't already lapsed, before signing with a professional manager, or you could end up giving so many rake-offs to different people who have helped you at various times in your career that you're left with nothing yourself (except law suits).

Will all my income go through the manager?

A proper manager will arrange to collect all booking fees, record royalties and songwriting royalties from publishers (not PRS fees though, if you're a member of PRS) plus royalties for you from the merchandising of goods bearing your name or picture of you, fees for television appearances, opening fetes and supermarkets, parts in films etc., etc. What he shouldn't get is a percentage of your income from *any* source, as this would include money you may earn or be paid completely outside the entertainment business (even in

theory such things as football pool winnings or legacies from rich relatives!).

What percentage will the manager take?

The manager will probably take around 15% to 20% of your earnings from the entertainment business. It may be more than that, though it could be on a sliding scale so that once you're earning £100,000 a year he isn't still getting as high a percentage as he was when you were earning £1,000 a year. If you are in the 'big time' then he will probably collect all your earnings himself and pay you your 80% at regular intervals. Similarly potential agents, record companies and so forth will know that they must approach him if they wish to make a deal with you. Until

you reach that stage you will often be approached by these people direct, and your contract will require you to put them on to the manager, even though you may be tempted to deal with them directly. Also you may be paid direct in which case you may be obliged to pass over all the money to the manager. You will get your share of it back a few months later. Again this may seem stupid from your point of view but such a situation should be borne in mind when you're signing the contract with the manager, and any changes should be spelled out.

Who pays for what?

If you're signing with a professional management then the chances are that they'll initially pay for everything, although the contract will make it clear that ultimately it will be you who pays. They'll probably sign you for several years (as with publishing contracts three to five is quite reasonable). They may then pay all your travelling expenses plus an allowance to you of so much per week while you're struggling. They won't pay you anything more than that until they have recovered from money earned by you all their expenses on you, and they may wish to keep you on a low 'spending allowance' per week for some time after you've started to be worth big money, until they're sure that their expenses will not for a longwhile exceed the income, leaving them out of pocket again.

All this is fine, and it's nice to know they have such faith in you. Obviously a lot of management companies lose a lot of money this way as they should never actually make you pay any of the expenses back (unless perhaps to buy yourself out of the contract). The biggest snag with such a large and benevolent organisation is that it usually has its own agency, recording and publishing companies to which you will be signed automatically, so that you need to make quite sure from someone independent of the management company, before you sign with them upon what terms you will be asked to give them your recording and songwriting services, and you will have to be quite sure of their trustworthiness.

Even with regular statements from your management to you and even though you know what they're paying you each week in allowances it could become almost impossible for you to work out just what they've spent on you, for you are very much in their hands. You could have hit after hit — the management may give you the money to go out and buy a Rolls or a new house, but are they still advancing you their money or actually paying you what you've earned? If they're honest then regular statements (say every quarter) should be sent to you showing exactly how much you've earned and how much they've spent on you, but regrettably you'll probably lose all track of how much you are owed if you become very successful.

What happens if a manager pays me an advance?

As we've said if you've been paid an advance, whether in cash or in the form of things bought for you or expenses paid, you can more easily lose track of what you are owed. Alternatively you may be fortunate enough to be earning so much already at the time of being offered an advance that you'd lose nearly all of it in tax. Nevertheless you should generally take the advance (if the deal is a good one anyway) as it represents money in your pocket. You know you've got it and unless the contract is very badly worded, you won't ever have to pay it back except gradually out of your earnings collected for you by the manager.

The guarantee is a different matter from the advance. Find out what happens if your earnings haven't reached the magic figure which is guaranteed by the end of the five years or whatever. The contract may just say that you are free and the deal terminates (big deal) or it may give the manager the right to keep you for a further term which may be the last thing you want. Worst of all it may even say that the contract continues ad infinitum until the figure has been reached, though this would be so crooked as to be almost laughable, and even if the manager has made you quite a lot of money you could almost certainly walk out of such an agreement after the initial period, as the courts would declare the contract to be unfair to you, representing a 'restraint' of your activities.

If all my money comes to me through one person or firm, how can I check up on their honesty?

You will do well to keep asking questions and not to let success go to your head (easier said than done). You can work out from this book very roughly what should be due to you if you have a million selling record, for

instance. Much more important however, once you're apparently successful is that you should at all costs have your own independent accountant. Even if you trust your manager implicitly it is better to have your finances sorted out by some competent person who is not recommended by and therefore possibly biased in favour of your manager. As well as sorting out your tax problems as a 'self-employed entertainer' or whatever, he can be asked every so often to audit the books of the manager. You should have the right under contract to look at the manager's accounts where they relate to you, and whereas you probably won't understand them, your accountant will.

Do I really need to read through contracts secured for me by my manager?

If you are signed to a manager who is not also a record company and a publisher he will probably have promised verbally to try to secure for you a recording and publishing deal as success in these fields will obviously be likely to further your career as a performer. Try not to be over-impressed if a manager gets you a recording or publishing contract, and always try to take it away and read it yourself and ask him questions. You might like to think that he couldn't possibly make a bad deal and he will certainly let you think that he's an expert in everything to do with the music business. Alternatively your contract

46

with him might say that he has the sole right to negotiate such a deal on your behalf and on terms which he considers to be advantageous to you. You might therefore think either that it isn't worth suggesting alterations or that you have no right to, especially if the signing is to be a formal occasion with a photographer and reporter from the music press present. Nevertheless you should make every effort to check the contract first. It may be a terrible deal which the manager had done mainly to impress you, or he may have been given a big advance payment for your services, and doesn't want you to know about it. Or he may simply know nothing about publishing or recording. Even the most professional of managers can still agree to a 'lousy' deal because of inexperience in a particular field.

How would I get out of a management contract?

This is the most important of our three 'how to get out of' sections, since if your manager turns out to be greedy, dishonest, or simply disinterested, then no matter how honest and hardworking your record company and publisher may be, all the money they pay to you may go via your manager. So if he fails to pay you, or does a bunk once you've had a successful record, tour or hit song then you end up with nothing at all.

The advice given under publishing and recording contracts also applies here. First try the friendly approach, offering if necessary to pay back part or all of any advance sums or expenses paid by him on your behalf. Then check renewals and royalty statements to see that these have all arrived on time. If you're not successful the manager will probably let you go, possibly subject to his retaining some interest in your future in the form of a very

small percentage of your future income for the rest of the duration of his contract. If you are successful then he won't want to let you go and you will need to go straight to a solicitor to assess the case on its merits. If you succeed in getting out, then the solicitor's fees will probably be money well spent.

If you have a good case, one stroke your solicitor can pull is to write to your record company, publisher etc. asking that royalties be paid direct to you in future. This should at least ensure that the manager doesn't get them even if you yourself don't actually get paid. Faced with two 'claimants' to royalties, record companies and publishers will have no option but to suspend payments until the dispute is settled, just in case it should go to court and the winner should sue them for having already paid all the royalties to the loser. Obviously this won't go on

forever and in fact you as the new claimant will probably have a year or so in which to prove that you should now receive these royalties, otherwise they will be once more paid to the original claimant.

AGENTS, AGENCIES AND PROMOTERS

There are the people to whom artists (or their managers) turn to find work for them, fix up concert tours and engagements and handle the work involved. It is a specialised field and in view of the high costs of travel and hotel bills plus hire and transportation of amplification, lighting and sets, this can be very big business indeed, especially for example, in the case of a group touring the USA.

Who are they and what do they do?

It is often difficult to say where the line should be drawn between an agent and a promoter. Until recently 'Agents' obtained licence to operate from Local Authorities for a pound or two a year but as from July 1976 and under the Employment Agencies Act of 1973 (designed primarily to regularise the activities of Employment Bureaux and Typing Agencies — but as with all laws, actually embracing all sorts of people and things not envisaged by their compilers) a performers booking agency has to obtain a business permit from the Department of Employment which costs around £50. This should reduce malpractice but strangely, actual 'Promoters' are not required to be licensed in the same way. If you are doubtful of an 'Agent' (whether you are dealing with him directly or not) you can now, at least, enquire as to whether he is properly registered to assure yourself that the fee you earn will be collected and paid to you. This is assuming that you do not actually collect it yourself in cash on the night and then pay over the agent's percentage to him later, which is often the case.

The principal function of a booking agent is precisely to obtain work for you as a live performer. If you are using one exclusive agency then they may secure bookings without prior reference to you and let you know later (but always in good time) when and where the venues are. Otherwise they will check you beforehand as to whether you are free and wish, at the price, to play at certain venues, though this is obviously less satisfactory from the agency's point of view. Once it is verbally agreed, they will send you a form of agreement to complete. An example of this is included later in this book under 'examples of contracts' together with some notes about the terms.

The agent's commission should be between 10% and 15% of the fee for each booking. If you have a manager, then of course he will deal with the agency or agencies on your behalf although you can obviously deal directly with an agency, or direct with the venues themselves quite satisfactorily (though not if you were first introduced to those venues by the agency, who will require you to go through them again for future engagements). A form of simple agreement between you as an artist and a venue is also included in the 'examples of contracts' section. Naturally if you are contacted directly by venues you will see no point in paying either a manager or an agent a percentage of this money. For this reason there is no reason to tie yourself either to a manager or to an agency if as a semi-professional you have as much work as you want already. If you are a member of the Musician's Union, then it is important to ensure that the agent does not find you engagements which pay less than the Union's minimum rates. Even if you are not a Union member, then you should use these rates as a guide to whether you are being paid a reasonable amount for the job. On a semi-professional basis, it is inevitable that a competent 2 or 3 piece group will attract a bigger fee per man in small social clubs, pubs, etc. than a larger group providing roughly the same sort of performance.

How much per appearance should I be worth?

This really is the hardest question of all to answer, because there are so many factors to take into account. It's where managers and agents really earn their money, as they should know exactly how much they can get for your services in every situation. Most solo pop artists start their careers with groups these days, as they couldn't possibly start from scratch employing backing musicians or buying or hiring all the necessary equipment themselves. A normal group starting up should be able to equip themselves with tolerable second-hand gear (a good PA, public address system, being the most important item) for about £1,000 or with good, really reliable second-hand gear for about £2,000 (two or three times that amount for good new equipment). If they're prepared to play music to dance to and can get bookings at pubs, working mens' clubs, wedding receptions etc., the going rate for these should be about £80-£130. An act doing a residency at a venue or one whose services are in demand locally should get £150 or more, nationally £250 or more. A straight "pop" group with a recent hit (regardless of line-up) should get over £1,000 a night, much more if they consolidate their success and they can still be worth that long after the hit if they remain crowd-pullers. The biggest snag is if you're a top 'heavy' group, for the expense of putting on a one night performance can end up the best part of your £10,000 plus fee. The biggest acts can of course command thousands of pounds per booking, and for foreign tours, but amounts vary so much that no accurate guide can be given. At the lower end of the scale it is worth bearing in mind that as long as the instruments and voice are in tune then sheer reliability — always turning up on time, having the voice clearly audible, avoiding technical hitches, feedback etc. — can be more important to the securing of regular well-paying engagements than real musical talent!

A group playing at social clubs, parties, dinner-dances, pubs etc who are prepared to play (and take their breaks) when asked, to turn the volume down (or occasionally up) when asked, to look presentable, to set up and pack up quickly and to vary the programme to suit the age or taste of the audience are certainly more likely to be re-booked. It is another plus for the group if they have their own stage lights and taped music to play during intervals — some small venues lack these facilities, though the club or whatever might draw the line at strobe lights, dry ice and pyroflashes. It is worth remembering that, although these types of venue can only pay a certain fee for music regardless of the number of musicians in the line-up, they will certainly pay much more over Christmas and especially on New Year's Eve, when demand for music exceeds the supply.

GENERAL QUESTIONS
AND ANSWERS

GENERAL QUESTIONS AND ANSWERS ON THE MUSIC BUSINESS

How long must I wait for my royalties?

Royalties can take a very long time to reach you from the time when they are first earned. Using the example of overseas publishing royalties on record sales, if a song you write is a hit in say the USA in Autumn 1984 the American record company waits until the end of their next accounting period before paying the USA record royalty collecting agent. At the end of the collecting agent's accounting period it pays the USA publisher, who waits until his next accounting to pay the UK publisher. At *his* next accounting, and not before, he pays you, or if you have a manager then he pays your manager, who a few months later pays you. Accountings are generally half-yearly, so for each link in the chain you might be waiting up to another six months for your royalties. In the above case it could be as late as the end of 1986 or beginning of 1987! The moral of this is don't go on a spending spree as soon as you learn that you have a hit song in the USA or other foreign parts as you may be waiting years for the money, and don't assume also that your publisher in this case is being dishonest (or your record company or your manager in similar cases). Just try to keep a track of where your biggest earnings should be coming from and be patient.

Where will my biggest earnings come from?

In terms of straightforward UK earnings for a UK artist/songwriter, unless the songs become standards, in which case they will go on earning enormous sums year after year then artist royalties on hits will bring in more money than songwriting. Over the period when you have the hits, your earnings from live appearances, provided you were capitalising on your popularity, will be even greater.

The best places in the world in which to have a big hit moneywise are firstly, needless to say, the USA, then Japan, West Germany and the UK followed by France, Italy, Brazil (if you can get the money out) and the other 'markets' such as Australia, Holland, Belgium, Canada, Scandinavia and South Africa. Owing to the ineffectiveness of copyright protection and consequent lack of exploitation, large areas like the rest of Africa, India, the 'Iron Curtain' countries, the Middle and Far East and much of South America can be almost ruled out when working out where money will be coming from. In most of these places there exists copyright protection of sorts but it is often not rigidly enforced, many foreign records being imported and sold, along with 'bootleg' and 'pirate' recordings, illegal copies of hits from the USA or UK. In Hong Kong one can even take a record into a record shop and for a small charge have a tape recorded copy made in total disregard of the songwriters' and artists' rights and those of the publisher and record company. There are places in the world, mainly in the poorer parts, where money may have been collected for you and put into a bank account in your name. Contracts with publishers and record companies sometimes specify this because 'Exchange Control' regulations prevent money being sent out of the country.

This means that sooner or later you will have to go there to spend it, fine if it's Spain but not so funny if it means paying your fares to and from Brazil.

In your favour in all of this is the fact that outside the enormous Japanese market in which millions of Japanese rush out to buy almost solely Japanese records by local artists, British and American pop music, in the English language is supreme all round the world. This is borne out by the tendency for many Continental-European artists to perform local songs with English lyrics in the Eurovision Song Contest, believing that this will increase their chances of success.

What happens if they don't pay me as agreed once I've played?

Provided that you arrived on time and played, or were prepared during the time stated, just try writing polite letters followed by stronger letters from a solicitor if it's worth it. You can always ask a solicitor if he'll tell you what his charge would be for such a letter. It might well be worth it. If you were late or unable to perform for the length of time expected once you've arrived then the management of the venue might deduct a proportion of your fee for this, which is not unfair provided that the proportion deducted is not much greater than the proportion of the agreed time which you missed.

What happens if I agree to perform somewhere and am unable to turn up?

If there is a good reason, then apologise and the management of the venue is not likely to do very much with the exception of not book-

ing you again. Obviously you'll probably know a short time beforehand that you can't make it and will tell them immediately. They could ask you to supply a replacement, but only an agency can reasonably be expected to do this. The only alternative is to offer to perform on another date, perhaps for a reduced fee.

Is it illegal to record TV programmes or records on a tape or video recorder?

Yes, especially if you were to make copies and sell them, even to friends. This would be "piracy". Although manufacturers of cassette and video recorders often seem to be inviting people to do this, it is illegal to record any copyright material without the permission of the copyright owners. In the case of radio or television programmes, this means the BBC or IBA or producer of the programme, the owner of the recordings and the publisher of the songs being performed, as well as any musicians or actors, script writers, producers or others whose services were not "bought out" by any of the first three. The taping of records still affects the rights of the record company and publishers. The levy on the price of blank audio and video cassettes which the music industry has pressed for for a number of years is intended to compensate these rights owners for part of their losses through home taping. Although this penalizes the small number of people who only ever use cassettes and videos for personal home

movies, recording their own voices etc. this seems the fairest overall solution.

What can I do if the venue cancels an agreement?

Generally where an agent has dealt with the venue the agency will have put into the contract a clause to the effect that a cancellation fee of perhaps half the agreed fee is payable if the engagement is cancelled by the venue less than a week before it was due to take place. If you are dealing directly with the management of the venue yourself and have made no mention of cancellation fees then you will simply have to regard it as bad luck, and avoid making further bookings for that venue.

Can I assume that a printed contract will be 'standard' and therefore reasonable?

It is worth noting that if you are offered a printed contract then the company offering it is less likely to let you have anything altered in your favour as the terms are probably pretty standard. Against this the terms are less likely to be prepared specially to your disadvantage as they could possibly be with a typed xeroxed contract. Obviously the only real answer is to read it. It may contain a 'schedule' setting out the royalties and the duration on the outside with other important details, and contain a lot of small print on the inside, or vice versa. If this is the case then read the small print as well as the large. An apparent high royalty and short duration may be totally different once the small print is applied.

If the contract is typed, or altered if it's printed, make sure that all the copies are identical and that the meaning of all the wording is completely definite especially where it relates to duration and royalty rates. If not then whoever is signing you up could claim, in the event of a dispute, that the real intention or wording was something different from what you understood it was at the time of signing, and as he can produce a copy of the agreement signed by you this could present you with problems.

What happens if I lose my copy of the contract?

Just a general cautionary word about being methodical where contracts are concerned.

Even if your manager has secured the contracts for you and has copies himself, always

try to keep a copy of every contract you sign and of every letter you write on the subject of contracts, as you're never quite sure when you might need to produce them. If you lose a contract you can ask the other party (publisher, record company or whoever) for a copy to be made of their copy, and most companies will do this quite readily. A crooked company could always take the opportunity to alter the terms in its favour, but this isn't very likely.

What does the Musicians Union do and should I join?

This body is very active in ensuring an increasing supply of work for musicians and reasonable fees. They have constantly campaigned to ensure that radio stations do not play records *all* day, so that a proportion of the airtime is devoted to live music. They have required that all musicians appearing on such television programmes as 'Top of the Pops' either must play live or, if they wish to mime, must mime to a re-recording of their record (making more work for musicians, orchestras and choirs). A basically amateur musician would not need to join the Union, but all musicians would be well advised to do so. The Union lays down certain minimum rates for all session musicians, at a specific rate for a three hour session plus extra for doubling on another instrument, extra for porterage, overtime, etc. There are also set rates for recording for broadcasts etc. The record companies have agreements with the MU whereby they agree to pay MU rates for all their sessions, and you should certainly be a member if you wish to start doing sessions regularly – the Union is in any case working in your interests. This would mean agreeing not to play for less

than Union rates, but this is unlikely to worry a good working musician or a "pop star" whose interests the MU is safeguarding. Membership costs annually a few pounds upwards to a certain maximum depending upon the member's earnings as a musician. The address to write to for information is 60/62 Clapham Road, London SW9.

How can I protect my stage name or group name?

If you have not yet achieved any sort of national recognition and another artist or group appears and becomes successful with an identical or very similar name to yours then there is really not a great deal of point in sticking to your name if members of the public hearing the name will immediately think of the other, successful, act. If the other act were to feel it necessary, they could probably stop you using your name if the courts of law felt that it would mislead the public, and it would be unlikely that you could reverse the process and stop them using theirs, even if you had been using yours much longer. You could register the name just as one would register the name of a business, but unless you were already successful you would probably be unable to prevent another act using the name and would just have to regard it as very bad luck. When the Shadows first rose to fame with Cliff Richard in the late 50's they were prevented from using their original name, 'The Drifters', by the American group, already successful, of that name, although if the Shadows had never found fame, their use of the name 'Drifters' would probably never have been questioned. Incidentally be sure not to chose a stage name which is too ephemeral i.e. which may sound outdated after a year of two. This is especially the case where an artist actually decides to change his name by deed-poll to his stage name.

What can I do if my real name is Paul McCartney?

Well this really is bad luck. Obviously you'd be silly to try to use it, as no-one would dare book you or record you under that name for fear of audiences and record buyers thinking they were going to hear your famous namesake, and in fact the manager of the well-known artist would probably take you to court over it anyway if you used the name as your stage name. William Richard or Cliff Smith would certainly be quite acceptable on the other hand.

If a group splits up, who owns the name?

Regrettably there is no straightforward answer to this question. It may be that the members will work something out between them. It may be that they themselves do not actually 'own' the name at all. If the record company or manager suggested it there may be something in the contract whereby he reserves the right to the name, in which case if all the members of the group leave together or one by one, they can be replaced by an entirely new group with the same name. This prospect is something to question managers or record companies about when signing with them, as it is probably the last thing you want.

Can I stop anyone else recording or performing in my style or manner?

Unfortunately not, unless they are actually deceiving the public into thinking that they're really you, which is known as 'passing off', in which case your manager or record company, if you have them, will take action against the other artist. Otherwise there's nothing at all that you can do. If you come up with a 'great new sound' then the chances are that all sorts of people will copy it, and unfortunately there's nothing you can do to stop this either.

Do I have to pay to perform other people's songs in public?

Singers or groups normally should never be charged for performing a song in public (even on television). The venue where the performance is taking place should be licensed by the PRS as we have discussed earlier, and if it's not, then that isn't the fault of the performer who, having been booked to appear, can reasonably assume that the venue is properly licensed.

If you yourself wish to put on an open air concert in a field, or just to play records at a fete on the vicar's lawn then for all such performances to which the public has access in places which are obviously not regularly licensed for the playing of music permission should be sought from the PRS's general licensing department. Religious services do not however require a licence, although if a song of yours were to be broadcast on television or radio as part of a religious service

then this would be no different from any other broadcast as far as the payment of performing fees is concerned.

Who are publicists and what do they do?

Obviously from the name, they are involved with publicity. Some managers, record companies and the like make use of independent publicists, either to generate publicity for themselves or their artists or to release 'statements' to the press about new artists signed, forthcoming tours arranged and suchlike. Other larger organisations have their own 'press offices', to arrange the company's advertising. One feature of their activities is the 'publicity stunt'. These are overdramatised or largely ficticious stories of stars getting married, getting divorced, moving

abroad, narrowly escaping death in car crashes, denying taking drugs and so forth.

What can I do personally to gain publicity?

If you are just a local artist or group and you wish to publicise yourselves then the possibility of your making a record is usually enough to interest the local press. The most basic piece of publicity is to have small but attractive cards with your name and what you do plus your address or just phone number to give to enquirers or to leave at venues where you have played. A few hundred of these will cost no more than a few pounds or so and are an absolute must. If you have a manager, then his name and number ought to go on the cards, as well as yours. Advertisements in local papers are possible, for around £5 or so per week, and often under an 'entertainers' heading which will generally list only advertisements for children's entertainers and mobile discotheques. The other obvious means of attracting publicity is through posters, but you need to be very careful that you do not fall foul of the local authority by putting these up where you shouldn't.

How binding are verbal agreements?

A very straightforward verbal agreement between you and for instance a publisher made in the street in the presence of a couple of mutual friends, to give him your next composition on his usual terms in return for £10 advance, whilst not in itself an assignment of the copyright in that song, is nevertheless a perfectly valid agreement to which either of you should be able to hold the other. If his terms turned out to be much less good from your point of view than you might reasonably have expected, then probably he would have to improve them to what a court would regard as usual in the business before he could hold you to the contract, unless of course you already knew beforehand that his standard terms were not very good.

A verbal agreement is never normally good enough on its own and should always be confirmed by a written one. It is simply impossible to cover all reasonable eventualities in a verbal agreement even though you might think it satisfactory at the time. You might agree with someone over the telephone to play at his venue for £80 on a certain night from 10 pm until 12 pm, but what happens if he claims not to have realised that you expected a break during that period or if it turned out that he expected a singer and you were just an instrument combo. Such snags are much more easily ironed out where a written agreement exists.

Above all, note that on any agreements at or near the bottom there will be wording such as 'this agreement represents the total agreement between the two parties and can only be altered in writing'. If the person offering you such an agreement says, whilst explaining it, such phrases as 'Oh don't worry about that', 'this never happens' or 'obviously we'll up the royalty after a little while' you cannot hold him to any of this, and must ask him to have the contract altered to cover these things or else sign it at its face value.

Is it always illegal to make copies of music without permission?

Assuming that we are not talking about your own unpublished compositions, then there are no circumstances under which it is legal to make copies of music, even for purely personal use. Many publishers subscribe to a "code of fair practice" for individuals, schools etc. to make a few copies, usually for study. Others may permit this on request if copies are not sold or used for other purposes.

In what ways might VAT affect me?

Value Added Tax is payable on a great many goods and services in the UK and many other countries. The only person who cannot claim it back in some way is the 'consumer' at the end of the line (thus each member of the chain in the production and sale of a record can claim some of the tax he has paid back by collecting tax himself from the next person in the chain until it is eventually the record buyer who pays the appropriate tax on the cost of a record. There is no VAT on the cost of sheet music or books.

If you are 'in the business' say as a musician then you can register for VAT. You can claim VAT from record companies, publishers and the management of venues at which you perform. If you are registered then the first two of these bodies are obliged to pay you the additional VAT on top of your royalties if you send them an invoice for it quoting your VAT registration number. At venues you can charge this if you ask for it initially together with your fee, but if you forget then you will be in the embarrassing position of having to go back to them and ask for it. Although all this VAT you have collected is payable periodically by you to the government, you can, before paying it, deduct (if registered) all the VAT you yourself have had to pay on new instruments, stage clothes, tape recorders, manuscript paper in fact anything which was reasonably necessary to the pursuit of your musical career.

All this may sound fine but it does have to be properly worked out by your accountant (you'll need to have one if you wish to register for VAT). It is often worth registering though you may not at first have thought that it would be, but it would require an accountant to tell you whether in your particular circumstances this would be a worthwhile step.

Who gets what from the sale of a record?

As only the copyright royalty is a fixed percentage in the UK (6¼%) and because record companies do not always make, press and distribute their own records, but use outside companies frequently for part of this, especially in the case of "independent" record labels, it is difficult to be precise, but the following approximate percentages are a guide:

Pressing (the actual disc)	20%
Labels/white sleeves	2%
Copyright royalty	6%
Artist royalty	10%
Other royalty (producer)	2%
Record company/wholesaler margin	34%
Retailer margin	26%
	100%

All of this excludes tax (VAT). The record dealer (retailer) seems to be taking a large cut, but remember that he has paid out initially to buy the records from the wholesaler (often one of the major record companies' offshoots) and although from time to time distributors have allowed retailers to return 5% of records ordered in return for a credit note, basically the dealer takes the enormous risk of not selling the record. If no-one wants it, a piece of grooved plastic is remarkably worthless (just take a look through a second-hand record dealer's racks, where brand new recent deleted singles can be 10p or less!)

The record company itself seems to get a large percentage if it is doing its own distribution (it costs minor record companies around 15-20% of the retail price to have this done). However out of this apparent profit must come all their overheads as well as the costs of making the recording and the costs of advertising which can be very high (hundreds of pounds for even a half-page advertisement in the musical papers).

Copyright (for recording artists)

Just as there is a copyright in a song as soon as it exists in 'tangible form' (i.e. tape or manuscript etc.) there is also copyright in recordings, even though they themselves contain someone else's copyright, namely the song which is recorded. The copyright in the recording lasts for 50 years from the end of the year during which the recording was first released. In fact there is also copyright in such things at TV programmes, which might well contain the copyright in recordings played in them which in turn contain the copyright in the songs on the records! The effect of this is that no-one else can video copy the TV programme for distribution or sale. Similarly although someone else can make records of a song which you have recorded and had released, nevertheless they couldn't make records of your own actual performance without permission from you or your record company.

The record company will put a P in a circle ' ℗ ' plus the year of release of the master tape on each of their records, plus the name of the original company producing the record (to comply with USA copyright laws).

What is important for you to note is that right from the start the copyright in the record belongs to the record company and not to you unless you produced the master recording yourself entirely at your own expense and the record company's rights are from a lease made by you. Otherwise it is their creation made by them and paid for by them.

How can I avoid looking oversuspicious of everyone?

All the while you are trying to sell yourself to an interested company you will obviously not want to appear too suspicious of their honesty, and consequently it's advisable to assume that any contract which they may eventually submit for you to sign will be a reasonable one. As long as you don't agree to anything definite you are always quite free to back out if you don't like the look of the contract. Do try, however, to have a signed contract with them before you actually begin working with them. Once money starts to be earned, you will only be able to stop it by recourse to law, if the contract they eventually offer you is not to your liking. In your favour in such a situation is the fact that until you have signed with them exclusively, you are free to go to any other company — a situation which no company wants. If you find yourself in such a situation you really should consult a lawyer who can evaluate the specific case on its merits.

What is an "at-source" publishing deal?

It has become quite common practice for a

group or artist to wait until they have secured a record company agreement, or better still until their first record shows signs of becoming a hit before negotiating a blanket songwriting deal with a publisher. In these circumstances they may be able to get a much larger advance royalty, and should be able to insist on an at-source royalty deal.

In normal agreements the writer is paid say 50% of what the publisher gets from abroad without actually spelling out what the publisher will get. If the publisher owns a company overseas he could divert all the money through that company and end up with only 10% to divide with the writer in the UK without breaking the agreement, though of course this would be totally immoral. In an at-source deal the total percentage of worldwide earnings will be stated. If this is 75%, then both the UK publisher and his sub-publisher in each foreign country must share the other 25%. This sort of figure is very low, but if a hit record is involved then publishers may consider such a deal. An alternative is for the UK publisher to pay say 80% of his receipts from sub-publishers and guarantee that they will pay 80% of their receipts from source. "Source" normally means total mechanical royalties but excluding collecting society commissions, as the foreign sub-publishers usually have no control over these – many cannot collect direct from record companies but must use the local collecting society.

Many publishers are simply not able to offer an at-source deal since they cannot be sure of doing overseas sub-publishing deals which will pay a high enough percentage for them to pay the writer what he requires without losing money. Only international publishing companies can normally do this. If the record fails to take off in the UK while the group are still searching for the best deal they may miss out of course. On the other hand if the record becomes a worldwide hit before a deal is made fees may be lost from various sources, so it pays not to be too greedy.

What should I know about video?

As a songwriter, the use of one of your songs in a video tape or disc equivalent of an LP will be licensed by your publisher, often through the MCPS at a rate agreed within the industry. This is rather complex but comes out at around the same percentage of the retail price on the sale of a "videogram" (the name for video tapes and discs) as on the sale of a record. This also applies to films which are reproduced on videograms and may contain one of your songs, but here if the

total amount of music used is small the total royalty is reduced in proportion. If the film was made before the emergence of video then the publisher's original synchronisation licence to the film company may have covered sale or hire of videos, in which case you may miss out. Royalties on videos which are released for hire tend to be fairly low, and you probably won't see anything from the hire of videos or films on a daily basis by many of the street corner video shops. Add to this the fact that many of the street videos sold are illegal pirated copies and you will see that songwriters and their publishers have not been making fortunes from this new medium.

As an artist you may very well be asked to make a video of yourself performing a single (or even an LP) purely as a promotional tool for your record company to use. This could be played on television pop programmes, sent abroad to interest foreign record companies or broadcasters in you etc. For this you will receive only a fee for your original performance. Many big name acts now produce their own videos, usually surrealistic, often very expensive and as much of an art form as the records they are promoting. Artist royalties on videos of you sold by your record company alongside the records and tapes will usually be at the same rate.

Many artists and groups find it useful to have a cheap video of themselves performing, made by a friend or freelance producer (these can be found in classified ads. in your local paper) to send to record companies, publishers and agents. This can cost very little and can make a big impression. If you wish to have copies made of your own videos for you to sell, as some artists and small production companies do, then the MCPS will guide you as to copyright requirements.

Have we made you feel that everyone is out to swindle you?

We hope not, because although you'll now know what pitfalls to avoid, it needs to be said that for every crook in the music business there are dozens of honest people and just because someone's contract could be interpreted as giving him the right to do all sorts of evil things to you, he very likely has no intention of doing any of them and maybe they were just thought up by his over-zealous lawyer or maybe he doesn't know how to alter them without the risk of losing all his rights. For all that, it's nice to know that the contract you've signed is a reasonable one, and really does set out what you had agreed to.

CONTRACTS

EXAMPLES OF CONTRACTS, WITH COMMENTS

In this section we have included examples of the various forms of agreement that you might be asked to sign as a songwriter, recording artist or performer. All the agreements are slightly shorter or more straightforward-looking than some with which you may be confronted, but this is to make them more easily understandable, and they contain all the necessary wording and necessary clauses in each case. Examples of royalty terms have generally been included, but you will know from our earlier comments what you could normally expect to get under such contracts in terms of royalty rates and hard cash.

Also shown is the form of notification that the Performing Right Society Ltd. requires in respect of a new song. These are filled in by the music publisher simultaneously with the song contract and must be signed by you as a songwriter before the publisher sends it to the PRS (except for an English lyric to a foreign song). In effect, that card then becomes the PRS's index card in respect of your song, so make quite sure that everything is correctly spelled (the song title, your name etc.) and that the division of performing fees shown is the same as on the contract with the publisher.

As we have said, artist management agreements can range from a scrap of paper appointing your next door neighbour as your manager, to a multipaged document with an international company which takes hours to read and even longer to understand. There is no such thing as a 'standard' artist management contract and these are usually prepared specially for each artist. There is nothing wrong with this provided that it is explained to you (preferably by someone who is competent to do this such as a solicitor who is independent both of your Manager and of his advisors) exactly what each part of the contract means — how much it ties you down and really how much you will eventually get from every £1 you earn. Try to think 'If I'm immediately successful, am I going to be happy to be bound by this contract'.

Right: Publishing contract for a specific song(s). For notes and comments on the terms of this agreement see under "Publishing Contracts" section.

Songwriter/Publisher contract for one song

An Agreement made this .... day of ....19...., between (a music publishing company/address) (hereinafter called "the Company") of the one part and ....

(a song writer/address) (hereinafter called "the Writer") of the other part

Whereby It Is Agreed as follows:-

1. IN consideration of the sum of .... (receipt of which the Writer hereby acknowledges) paid as an advance on account of the royalties provided for in Clause 4 hereof and of other good and valuable considerations the Writer hereby sells and assigns to the Company, its successors and assigns, the whole of the property, title, copyright and interest for all countries of the World in the original musical work(s) now entitled:

....

(hereinafter called "the Song")

including the right to collect royalties and fees outstanding for payment in respect of any uses of the Song prior to the date hereof, and including the right to secure copyrights, renewals and extensions thereof throughout the World, and all rights of whatsoever nature existing thereunder for the full terms thereof, including all rights which may hereafter be conferred by law upon the Song.

2. THE Writer hereby warrants that the Song is his own original work and that the rights herein assigned have not been previously assigned or pledged. The Writer hereby indemnifies the Company against any and all claims for alleged infringement by the Song of any other composition and against all expenses, settlements and damages arising from such claims. The Company is hereby irrevocably appointed the true and lawful representative of the Writer so far as may be necessary for the purpose of defending and/or instituting claims to maintain or establish the copyright in the Song.

3. THE Company is hereby authorised to make alterations in and additions to the Song at his discretion and to provide translations of the words or new lyrics in other languages.

4. THE Company agrees to pay royalties in respect of the Song to the Writer as follows:
   (a) 10% per copy of the recommended retail selling price of printed copies sold by the Company and paid for (pro rata in the case of song-books);
   (b) 50% of the net amount received by the Company of royalties in respect of the sale to the public of mechanical reproductions;
   (c) 50% of fees for miscellaneous uses;
   (d) 50% of royalties received by the Company from parties in foreign countries authorised by the Company to represent the interests of the Company in connection with the Song.

5. ROYALTY statements shall be made up to June 30th and December 31st in every year and sent to the Writer within 60 days thereafter accompanied by a remittance for the amount shown by such statements to be due and payable.

6. GENERAL performing fees and broadcasting fees shall be divided by the Performing Right Society Limited (hereinafter called "PRS") equally between the Company and the Writer.
   If the Writer be not a member or shall cease to be a member of PRS (or of one of its associated societies) then the performing rights in the Song shall be administered wholly by the Company (subject to its membership of PRS) who shall divide the general performing and broadcasting fees as provided in this Clause provided that the Company shall have received the shares appertaining to the Writer.
   The Writer hereby certifies that for the purpose of PRS rule 1(o) the Company is to be treated as exploiting the Song (otherwise than by publishing) for the benefit of the persons interested therein, to the extent indicated in the said rule.

7. THE Writer hereby conveys an irrevocable power of attorney authorising the Company, its successors and assigns, to file applications for renewal and renew and extend the copyrights in his name, and upon the issuance of such renewals, to execute proper and formal assignments thereof in his name, so as to secure to the Company, its successors and assigns, the renewal copyrights and extensions thereof.

8. THE Writer shall upon the request of the Company sign any further documents necessary to establish the Company's ownership of the rights hereby assigned.

9. IN this Agreement the Writer shall mean the party contracting with the Company whether that party be male or female, singular or plural.

As Witness the hands of the parties hereto the day and year first before written.

....
(the Writer)

....
for and on behalf of
(the Company)

Blanket Songwriting Agreement

An Agreement made this............ day of..............................197

....(hereinafter called "the Composer")

between ....

of the one part and ....

(hereinafter called "the Publisher") of the other part

WITNESSETH:

1. IN consideration of the sum of....................(receipt of which Composer hereby acknowledges) paid as an advance upon all royalties and fees provided for hereunder the Composer agrees to compose and write music and/or lyrics exclusively for and during the period of this Agreement for and on behalf of the Publisher and/or its related and/or associated companies and hereby undertakes to assign transfer and deliver to the Publisher its successors and assigns the whole of the property title copyright and other interest for all countries of the world in and to such music and/or lyrics and also in and to all compositions written heretofore by the Composer and not assigned to any other person or corporation subject to the rights of the Performing Right Society Ltd (hereinafter referred to as "PRS") but including reversion of the Performing Right in the event that such Society ceases to own the same. The Composer agrees not to render such services for any other person firm or corporation during the term of this Agreement without the prior written consent of the Publisher first obtained and not to act in his own behalf.

2. THE Publisher shall be entitled to secure copyright and renewals and extensions thereof throughout the world and all other rights of whatsoever nature existing for the full terms thereof whether such rights are now or hereafter known or conferred by law upon or in respect of compositions written by the Composer.

3. IN the event of the Composer collaborating with others in the composing of musical works the Composer shall then use his best endeavours to ensure that such other composers assign to the Publisher the copyright for all countries of the world in such musical works.

4. THE Composer warrants that all compositions assigned by him hereunder are and shall be original works and shall not infringe in any way the rights of third parties. The Composer hereby indemnifies the Publisher in respect of any claims demands and expenses arising from any breach of this warranty PROVIDED THAT the Publisher will not compromise or settle any claims without first consulting with the Composer in respect thereof and having proper regard to the views of the Composer in the light of the Publisher's knowledge and experience and in the light of legal advice received by it.

5. THE rights of the Publisher include the right to make alterations in and additions to the compositions the subject hereof and to provide new lyrics therefor and to make translations and new lyrics in foreign languages. The Publisher is also entitled to grant licences or authorise others to exercise its rights hereunder whether in whole or in part and to assign in whole or in part the compositions hereunder but the Publisher shall not be entitled to assign the whole burden of this Agreement without the prior consent of the Composer.

6. THE term of this Agreement shall be for a period of one year from the date hereof and thereafter may be extended at the Publisher's option for two further successive periods of one year each, each of such options to be exercised by the Publisher writing to the Composer at his last known address prior to the termination of the then current period, and paying to the Composer a further advance royalty sum of

7. IN respect of each composition the subject hereof the Composer shall upon demand execute a specific assignment in the form Schedule "A" attached hereto. The Composer shall further execute such forms as may be required by the Publisher for the PRS or other collection or copyright registration Society and Bureaux. The parties hereto agree to execute such further documents as may reasonably be required by the other to effect-uate the terms and conditions hereof.

8. THE Publisher undertakes to endeavour to promote such of the compositions the subject hereof which in its discretion it considers capable of development it being agreed that after (12) twelve months have elapsed from the date of specific song assignment herein before referred to the Composer may thereafter enquire of the Publisher in writing by registered mail whether any promotion has taken place in respect of the composition in question and in the event that the Publisher is unable to provide evidence of such promotion the Publisher shall forthwith reassign to the Composer the copyright in respect of such composition. For the purposes of this Agreement the expression "promotion" shall mean production by or on behalf of the Publisher of a demon-stration disc or tape or a printed edition of the composition or the commercial release of a record embodying the composition or the issue of a licence in respect of sound film use of the composition.

9. ALL costs incurred by the Publisher in the development of compositions acquired hereunder by the Publisher including but not limited to the making of top line copies demonstration recordings, printing, promo-tion and advertising expenditure shall be at the expense of the Publisher and the Composer shall not be charged with the whole or any part thereof.

10. (i)The Publisher agrees to pay royalties in respect of the compositions acquired hereunder to the Composer as follows:
    (a) Ten per cent per copy of the recommended retail selling price of printed copies sold by the Publisher and paid for and pro rata in the case of collective publications;
    (b) Fifty per cent of the net amount received by the Publisher of royalties in respect of the sale to the public of mechanical reproductions, fees for miscellaneous use (except performing and broadcasting as specified hereunder) royalties from foreign affiliated and associated companies of the Publisher or from persons firms and corporations authorised by the Publisher to publish editions of the composition.

10. (ii) General performing fees and broadcasting fees shall be divided by the PRS equally between the Publisher and the Composer subject to any allocation for orchestral arrangements or lyrics in accordance with the rules of PRS for the time being in force. The Composer hereby certifies that for the purposes of PRS Rule 1(o) the Publisher is to be treated as exploiting the compositions (otherwise than by publishing) for the benefit of the persons interested therein to the extent indicated in the said rule. If the Composer be not a member of PRS (or one of its associated societies) or if the Composer shall cease to be a member of PRS (or one of its associated societies or of its successor) then and in that case the performing rights in the compositions shall be administered wholly by the Publisher (subject to its membership of PRS) who shall divide the resultant performing fees and broadcasting fees (to the extent to which the Publisher shall have received the share appertaining to the Composer) as provided in this paragraph.

11. THE royalty statements shall be made up to June 30th and December 31st in each year to include all receipts by the Publisher in that period and sent to the Composer within ninety days of such dates and shall be accompanied by a remittance for the amount shown by such statements to be due and payable.

12. NO alleged breach of this Agreement which is capable of remedy shall be or be deemed a fundamental breach hereof unless the party complaining shall have given notice in writing to the other specifying such breach or alleged breach and the same shall not be remedied within a period of sixty days.

IN WITNESS WHEREOF   the parties have hereunto set their hands the day and year first before written.

SIGNED by the said COMPOSER ....

        in the presence of: ....

SIGNED by the said PUBLISHER ....

        in the presence of: ....

The pro's and con's of signing one of these agreements are set out in the "Songwriting" section of the book, but the following is a simplified version of the actual agreement, clause by clause, saying very basically what each one means. Even the most frightening and complicated contract can become quite easy to understand once each clause is analysed. The "Schedule A" mentioned in clause 7, by the way, is just a blank specific song contract like the one we have reproduced.

AN AGREEMENT made this .... day of ....19......between ....and the Honest Music Pub. Co. Ltd. in which the following is agreed:

1. PUBLISHER pays you a sum of money to write songs exclusively for him for a certain time. Publisher will have all the rights in the songs except the performing right (P.R.S. owns this and pays you and publisher separately). If you want to give another publisher a particular song, you must ask first.

2. SIMPLY states again that Publisher has all rights to songs.

3. If you have a co-writer you must try to get him to assign his part of each song to the Publisher.

4. YOU guarantee that your songs will be original, and if someone sues Publisher because you've lifted someone else's song, Publisher will consult you before taking legal action.

5. PUBLISHER can have foreign lyrics written to your song or alter it around a bit (He'll usually ask you first). He can give your songs to foreign publishers in different countries, but he can't sell your exclusive services for the next four years to another publisher, eg the Dishonest Pub. Co. Ltd., without asking you first.

6. PUBLISHER can renew the agreement before the first one year expires for another year, then another year after that. He may have to pay you a further advance each time.

7. YOU agree to sign anything else necessary to ensure that your songs are definitely assigned to the Publisher.

8. IF Publisher does nothing with one of your songs you can ask for it back a year after you signed the specific contract for it.

9. YOU won't be required to pay anything to Publisher to exploit your song.

10. i Simply states what royalties the Publisher will pay you — 10% of selling price of sheet music and half record royalties and miscellaneous royalties in UK and half of what he gets from foreign publishers.
    ii P.R.S. will pay you your half of the performing fees direct if you're a member. If not, then they'll pay your half to the Publisher to pay to you.

11. PUBLISHER will account to you twice a year.

12. SHOULD you claim that the Publisher had broken the agreement (eg by not paying royalties until 91 days after June 30th) he has another 60 days in which to remedy that before you can sue him.

IN WITNESS WHEREOF etc. etc.

Recording Contract

An Agreement

made this .... day of .... 19 ....

between .... (a recording company) of ....

(address) (hereinafter referred to as "the Company") of the first part, and .... (a recording artist)

of .... (address) (hereinafter referred to as "the Artist") of the second part

WITNESSETH as follows:-

1. THE Artist shall for the period of one year from the date hereof attend at such places and times as the Company shall reasonably require and render to the best of his skill and ability and to the satisfaction of the Company such performances whether alone or in company with one or more other artists as the Company shall elect for the purpose of reproduction thereof on any sound recordings including but not limited to master tapes, cinematograph films, film sound tracks and video tapes or any other recording device now or hereafter known, derivatives of which may be sold to the public.

2. THE Company agrees to utilise the recording services of the Artist to produce recordings in sufficient quantity to enable the Company at its discretion to place on sale to the public a minimum of four record sides or the equivalent thereof during each year of this agreement.

3. THE Company shall specify the musical works to be recorded hereunder but at its discretion may consult with the Artist and give due consideration to his wishes.

4. THE Artist undertakes that he will not without the prior written consent of the Company record during the term of this agreement under any name whatsoever alone or with others for any other party nor engage in, nor knowingly permit the manufacture, distribution or sale by anyone other than the Company of records embodying any performance by the Artist, nor will he for a period of three years following the termination of this agreement record any musical work recorded hereunder for any other party whereby recordings of such musical works may be reproduced for sale to the public.

5. IN consideration of the payment hereinafter set forth the Artist hereby grants to the Company or its licensees the right for all countries of the World to manufacture, advertise, sell or otherwise make use of recordings embodying the Artist's performances recorded hereunder upon such terms and conditions as the Company or its licensees may determine. The Artist hereby assigns and transfers to the Company or its licensees all rights in his performances as embodied in such recordings including but not limited to the sole and exclusive right to perform publicly or to permit the public performance by means of radio broadcast rediffusion service or otherwise of the Artist's performances hereunder. The Company or its licensees shall have the sole right to determine the type, quality, release date, labels, trade marks or trade names and all other matters connected with the manufacture, distribution and sale of records derived from recordings made hereunder.

6. THE Company shall pay all costs incurred by it in the production of the recordings to be made hereunder and all such recordings shall be and shall remain the sole and exclusive property of the Company.

7. THE Artist hereby warrants and represents that he has full power and authority to enter into this agreement and that he is not now subject to any other agreement or agreements which may in any way conflict with any of the terms of this agreement and the Artist indemnifies the Company against any claims by third parties that any of the rights granted by the Artist to the Company hereunder infringe the rights of such third parties.

8. AS remuneration for his services hereunder the Artist shall be entitled to a royalty (hereinafter referred to as 'the Royalty') at the rate hereinafter specified in respect of each record incorporating the Artist's performances hereunder and sold by the Company or by any party authorised by the Company and in respect of which the Company receives payment. The Royalty shall be calculated on 90% of sales less local and national taxes or duties. In respect of any records incorporating the performance or performances of the Artist together with any other artist who receives royalties for his performances, the Royalty shall be divided by the total number of artists including the Artist so performing in such records and in respect of any record incorporating separate performances by other artists, the Royalty shall be reduced in the same proportion as the number of the Artist's performances hereunder (alone or in conjunction with others) bears to the total number of separate performances contained in such record.

The Royalty shall be computed in the national currency of the place of sale but if the proceeds of a foreign sale shall be paid in the United Kingdom in sterling then the Royalty shall be paid at the same rate of exchange as that at which the exchange into sterling took place. The Company shall not be obliged to pay any royalty in respect of any foreign sale where, by virtue of currency restrictions, the Company is unable to obtain payment, but if it shall be lawful the Company shall endeavour at the request of the Artist to pay any royalty due in respect of such foreign sale into a separate bank account to be opened in such foreign country in the name of the Artist.

9. THE Royalty shall be at the Following rates:

(i) in respect of records sold by the Company in the United Kingdom and Eire a sum equal to 8% of the the recommended retail selling price (excluding tax);

(ii) in respect of records sold in all other countries and from parties authorised by the Company to make and sell records, a sum equal to 4% of the selling price in relation to which the Company receives payment from its licensees or agents.

(iii) in respect of records sold at a reduced price or through a record club mail order enterprise or similar organisation or in respect of sales of the so called low price "budget-line" records a sum equal to 50% of the specified royalty for the country of sale, however no royalty shall be payable in respect firstly of records which are distributed in not unreasonable quantities to members of any club operation as an inducement to obtaining further members of such club operation or records distributed as "bonus" of "free" records or secondly of records distributed by any club operation for any purpose and in respect of which that club operation is not paid or thirdly of records in "flimsy" form distributed free for advertising purposes.

The Royalty in sub-clauses (i) and (ii) shall apply during the term hereof but shall increase respectively to 10 % and 5 % in respect of records originally released for sale during the first period of extension hereof and respectively to 12 % and 6 % in respect of records originally released for sale during the second period of extension hereof or thereafter.

10. ACCOUNTS between the Company and the Artist shall be made up to 30th day of June and 31st day of December in each year and the Company shall pay to the Artist sums due to him at his last known address within 60 days thereafter accompanied by a statement showing how such monies were made up.

11. THE Company shall have options to renew this agreement for two separate and successive periods of one year each upon sending notice to the Artist in writing to such effect at his last known address prior to the termination of the then current term of the agreement provided that the Company shall have fulfilled its commitment to the Artist under Clause (2) hereof.

12. THE Company shall have the sole right to use and allow others to use and publish throughout the World the Artist's name, pseudonym or joint name, photographs, likeness and biographical material in any manner whatsoever for advertising purposes in connection with the promotion and distribution of records derived from the recordings to be made hereunder.

13. IN the event of the Artist's death or the Artist suffering deterioration or loss of voice or musical ability or for any other reason beyond the Artist's control whereby the Artist may become unable to fulfil his obligations to the Company hereunder then the Artist or his Estate will continue to be entitled to receive royalties hereunder in respect of the sale of records derived from the recordings then completed.

14. IF the Artist shall be a group then it is agreed that they will inform the Company in writing immediately upon any change in the personnel of the group and that they undertake to make any person joining the group as a regular member of the group fully aware that the group has entered into this agreement and that such new member will be required to acknowledge that he has read and understood this agreement and agrees to become bound by it. Notwithstanding any change in the personnel of the group it is understood that the total royalty hereunder in respect of each recording shall remain at the rate specified and will be divided amongst all those persons who are bound by this agreement as members of the group at the time of such recording. Any member leaving the group will remain bound by the terms of this agreement as though they related to him as an individual artist unless released specifically from this agreement by the Company.

15. FOR the purpose of this Agreement the word "records" shall mean any form of physical embodiment of sound whether with or without visual images manufactured by any method now or hereafter known from recordings produced hereunder and released for sale to the public and "the Company" shall mean not only the Company but also its successors and assigns and "the Artist" shall mean the party contracting with the Company whether that party be male or female, singular or plural.

16. THE Artist's execution of this agreement shall be regarded as the requisite consent required under the provisions of the Performers' Protection Act 1958, 1963 and 1972 or any other consent to record required from the Artist by Statute or otherwise from time to time.

17. THIS Agreement shall be construed in accordance with the laws of England.

IN WITNESS whereof the parties hereto have hereunder set their hands the day and year first before written.

SIGNED by the Artist ....

                                                                                                    signed by

                                        ....

                                                                                    for and on behalf of the Company

Left and above: Recording contract. For notes on the terms of this agreement see under "Recording Contracts" section.

Artist/Manager long-term agreement

Here is the sort of general management agreement which you may well be offered. These are the least 'standard' sort of agreements and both the wording and the terms vary enormously. Unlike other agreements shown here this particular example is one which you definitely wouldn't sign without substantial alteration, but it is included because it is very likely the sort of deal which you may be offered, and we have made comments on the terms, pointing out which are perfectly acceptable and which should be altered at all costs. Many management contracts are much longer than this (often many pages long) but they are generally only covering, in more detail, the same points as in this agreement.

Clause 1 is quite in order, provided that the total initial term is not more than one or two years. Clause 2 is also OK — in fact it is unusual for any aspect of your musical career to be excluded from the manager's control — but is this what you want? Clause 3 is very dubious. The manager may mean no harm and you probably know about his plans for your recording and songwriting services but it could be construed that he has the right to assign your services under contracts not requiring your signature and you won't even see them. Some wording here to the effect that the terms of these agreements also being regarded as usual in the opinion of the artiste or his independent adviser and in any case requiring your counter-signature would remove any possibility of your being completely taken for a ride.

Under Clause 4 you are agreeing to do various things and you may notice that there is no clause to say what would happen if you didn't. The Manager may intend to withhold your royalties or simply terminate the agreement, but the contract doesn't give him the right to do this as any mention of it would probably make the contract seem 'oppressive' towards you, and should you make out a case for walking out of the agreement the manager probably couldn't stop you. All he undertakes to do is to use his 'best endeavours' to promote you — a vague phrase with no real definition, for who can really say what his best endeavours are? As to the actual wording, parts (i), (ii) and (iii) are normal, the key word in (i) being 'reasonably'. Sub-clause (ii) could be too restrictive for you. You could 'endeavour' to vary your act in accordance with the requests of the manager or some such phrase. Sub-Clauses (iv) and (v) are OK, but as we have said the contract doesn't specify what will happen if for instance you swear at pressman and drink to excess before each performance.

Clause 5 is fine. The commission figure as we have said should be around 20%. Clause 6 in this agreement would have to be changed, to safeguard you from financial ruin, to the effect that expenses will be paid by the manager and then deducted from sums due to you which he has collected under Clause 7, which itself is quite normal.

Clause 8 is fine — not all managers send statements and payments as often as monthly. Clause 9 and 10 are reasonable. Under Clause 9 you'll find yourself paying over to the manager a lot of money which he really apparently did nothing to earn, but he'll take his cut of this regardless, and that can be quite normal.

Finally Clause 11 gives him the right to renew the contract (though it should not extend the total length to over five years) if you have earned a certain large sum of money during the initial period. There is no catch here. If you've made that much money then you're obviously succeeding and that must in part be due to him. If you haven't made it then at least you have only been bound to him for a comparatively short time (a year or two) and unless you wish to continue with him for another year or two on the same sort of terms you can simply call it a day quite amicably and find a new manager. It is worth bearing in mind that very many artists have long and happy relationships with their management.

This Agreement is made this .... day of .... 19 ....

between ....

and ....

.... (hereinafter called "the Manager") of the one part

.... (hereinafter called "the Artiste") of the other part

WHEREAS the Artiste is engaged in the entertainment industry and is desirous of appointing a Manager as his sole and exclusive Manager in respect of his activities within the entertainment industry.

NOW THEREFORE IT IS AGREED as follows:-

1. THE Artiste hereby appoints the Manager and the Manager hereby agrees to act as sole and exclusive Manager to the Artiste throughout the World for the term of .... years from the date hereof, and thereafter as provided for under Clause 11 and undertakes to use his best endeavours to promote the professional standing of the Artiste.

2. THE Manager shall manage the whole of the Artiste's activities within the entertainment industry, including the arrangement for the making of recordings, songwriting agreements, public, television, broadcasting, theatrical and film performances, as the Manager shall deem necessary and advisable.

3. CONTRACTS arranged by the Manager in respect of the Artiste's services may be with persons firms or companies associated with the Manager provided that they shall be upon terms which in the opinion of the Manager are usual within the entertainment industry.

4. THE Artiste hereby agrees and covenants with the Manager as follows:

   i. that he will devote so much of his time and talent to the entertainment industry as the Manager may reasonably direct and act at all times in accordance with contracts concluded by the Manger on his behalf

   ii. that he shall conform to the Manager's requirements as to the presentation of his act and to the content thereof

   iii. that he will not act exercise or perform his talents for any person during the existence of this Agreement other than the Manager, and shall perform no engagements within the entertainment industry without the prior approval of the Manager, and shall refer to the Manager all enquiries and offers of employment

   iv. that he will arrive at all venues in good time for all engagements, and shall attend all rehearsals, Press calls, photographic and recording sessions and business appointments as the Manager may reasonably direct and will fulfil such to the best of his abilities

   v. that he will at all times conduct himself properly and soberly.

5. AS remuneration for his services hereunder the Manager shall be entitled to be paid a sum equal to .... % of the gross earnings of the Artiste from his activities within the entertainment industry, including but not limited to performance, appearance and acting fees, recording, film, writer's and composer's royalties and fees, payments for articles, books, scripts or reviews, advertising revenue and revenue from licensing or using the Artiste's name in connection with merchandise.

6. ALL expenses shall be borne by the Artiste personally, but the Manager may agree to advance certain sums from time to time.

7. ALL sums or payments due to the Artiste from his activities within the entertainment industry shall be paid direct to the Manager.

8. THE Manager shall render an account to the Artiste for any sums received by him during each calendar month, within 14 days of the end of such month, accompanied by a remittance for the amount shown to be due to the Artiste, after deducting any advances made, and any expenses incurred by the Manager necessarily on behalf of the Artiste and at his request.

9. THE Artiste shall from time to time produce to the Manager on request proof of such of his earnings and income as have been paid to him directly, but are actually receivable by the Manager hereunder, and shall forthwith hand over the same to the Manager.

10. THE Manager shall keep separate books of account relating to the Artiste and shall produce the same to him or his Agent at reasonable notice.

11. PROVIDED that the total sums due and payable to the Artiste hereunder shall have reached not less than £ ....,000 during the term hereof, then the Manager shall have the right to extend this agreement for a further period of .... years upon the same terms and conditions as herein contained by writing to the Artiste to such effect at his last known address prior to the expiry of the initial term of this agreement.

IN WITNESS WHEREOF the Artiste and Manager have hereunder set their hands the day and year first before written.

....

The Artiste

....

The Manager

Artist Venue Agreement (through an agency)

An Agreement
made this.........day of .... 19....... between........... ....
(hereinafter referred to as "the Management") of the one part and..........................
(hereinafter referred to as "the Artiste") of the other part

WHEREBY IT IS AGREED as follows:-

1. THAT the Management engages the Artiste and the Artiste accepts the engagement to appear as known at the following venue from the date(s) for the period and at the salary set forth below

Date(s) ....

Venue ....

Salary ....

2. IT is agreed that the Artiste shall arrive at .... and perform his/their usual and known act for a period of .... hours divided into .... sessions as arranged with the Management terminating not later than ....

3. THE Artiste shall not without the written consent of the Management perform at any other public place of entertainment within a radius of   miles of the venue during a period of .... weeks prior to and.........weeks following this engagement.

4. THE salary shall be payable by .... to ....

5. THE Management undertakes to provide adequate dressing room facilities for the Artiste.

AS WITNESS the hands of the parties hereto the day and year first before written.

....

for and on behalf of
   the Management

....

The Artiste

Here is the sort of agreement submitted to an Artist or to his manager for him to sign for a specific booking or series of bookings. ('Management here means the owners of the venue.)

This form of agreement is quite normal and acceptable. The ideal form of payment is 'by cash to the Artiste on the night', preferably before you perform, but normally afterwards. If a singer or group wishes to take more than just a couple of roadies to a venue (i.e. wives, girlfriends, hangers-on) it's just as well to check by phone beforehand.

The Clause in this particular form of agreement which you must watch out for is Clause 3. The radius is often about 15 miles, and if you are playing at different London suburbs every night for a week it is quite unreasonable for the management of one venue to make you

agree to this, especially when you are comparatively little-known and the venues are private functions and are several miles apart. In such a case, in law this would probably amount to a 'restraint of your trade' and be unenforceable, but it's much better to try to have it deleted before you perform, to save misunderstandings and bad feelings as it really only exists for public concerts where a good turnout would actually be noticeably affected by your being billed to play at another local venue at around the same date. Another clause which is often included is one in which you undertake that you will not deal directly with the venue in the future and thereby cut out the agency. As we have said this is quite understandable as it was through the agent that you came to know of the venue in the first place.

Simple agreement to perform at a venue

*If you are securing engagements yourself and are
dealing with a venue which is not regularly booking
acts, or where the management is a bit casual as to
paperwork, they may ask you to write and confirm
a phone booking, in which case the following is
really quite adequate in most cases; typed in
duplicate, signed by you and sent to the
management of the venue.*

```
                                        Artists address

                                        date


    Dear ..............

    This will serve to confirm that.............(the artist)

    is booked to perform at....................on...........

    ............(date) from..............until............

    with suitable breaks for a fee of £............. payable

    in cash on the night.

    If you are in agreement with this please sign in the

    place provided below, and return one copy to me.


    Yours sincerely,




    .................................
    (the Artist)
    read and agreed




    .................................
    (the Management)
```

PRS notification card

Title	I LOVE YOU			Duration of Work	
Description		**Share of Royalties**		**Publication Date**	
Instrumentation		Performing	Mechanical	not yet published	
Composer	Oscar WINNER & Novello A. WARD	3/12 each			PRS Use
Author	same as composers				
Arranger					
Publisher	THE HONEST MUSIC PUBLISHING CO. LTD.	6/12	100%		
Territory	WORLD				

Date of assignment from writer(s)   1st January 1984

Date of agreement between publishers

Each of the undersigned assigns to the Performing Right Society Ltd. (PRS) the performing right as defined by the Articles of the Society in all parts of the world and agrees to the division of royalties indicated.
†The writer(s) hereby certify that for the purposes of PRS Rules the publisher is to be treated as exploiting the work for the benefit of the persons interested therein. † († = † delete if inapplicable)

For and on behalf of the publisher   THE HONEST MUSIC PUBLISHING CO. LTD.

Date   2nd January 1984   Signature

Signature(s) of Writer(s)

Copyright notice on sheet music.

Remarks (including details of commercial recordings)

"A" side of forthcoming single release by "The Stars" on Hit Records HT 101

*If you are <u>not</u> authorised to give clearance for B, D or E please state to whom application should be made

Above: An example of PRS/MCPS Notification Card completed. The publisher would type this in before you were asked to sign it. The details are typical. The "duration" and "instrumentation" are not usually filled in for a straightforward three minute song, but should be shown if the piece is much longer. The section "If you are not authorised . . ." refers to the back of the MCPS's copy of the card (not illustrated) and to the publisher's authorisation of the MCPS to collect mechanical, synchronisation royalties etc. which may vary. Generally the publisher collects 100% of royalties paid by MCPS and pays the writer his share.

By way of illustrating how valuable it is to read and understand the small print in contracts, here is a contract which no-one in their right mind would ever sign. Some of the clauses are obviously ridiculous, but in most cases the jargon is exactly what you would expect to find in a perfectly reasonable contract; it has simply been changed around slightly (eg clause 5). In point of fact if you were to sign such a contract you would not be held to it purely because it is so unfair to you and ambiguous, but remember, just because a contract looks O.K. at first there could easily be something hidden away in it which makes it very unfavourable.

An Agreement made this   day of   19   between   and Dishonest Records Ltd.

WHEREAS the Artist is desperate to secure a recording contract of any sort and WHEREAS the Company is totally unscrupulous.

NOW IT IS AGREED as follows:

1. THIS agreement shall be for the period of 10 years or the life of the Artist whichever shall be the greater, during which time he shall render no services to any other party for any purpose whatsoever. The Company guarantees the Artist not less than £1,000,000 (one million pounds) within each year of this agreement and should this sum not be reached then this agreement shall continue until such figure is reached, in which event the company may renew it for a similar term.

2. THE Company shall have the right to re-name the Artist eg. Mantovani, Led Zeppelin, The Beatles, etc. and the Artist hereby indemnifies the company against any legal action by third parties resulting from the use of such names.

3. SUBJECT to the Company giving not less than ½ hour's reasonable notice, the Artist shall attend at such times and places as the Company shall decide, and failure to honour this or any other undertaking made by either party hereunder shall import the determination of all the Artist's rights under this or any other agreement, in addition to any remedy which the Company may (or may not) have at law. The Company shall use whatever methods it finds necessary to ensure that the Artist performs to the best of his ability.

4. THE royalty payable to the Artist shall be 1% of the retail selling price of Master Tapes rising annually till it reaches 1½% of the wholesale selling price less taxes and other deductions which the Company may decide to make based on 90% (the figure customary in the industry) of all records returned as faulty or distributed free to any club operation.

5. IN the event of the Company releasing the Artist's performances on the so-called "normal", "full-price", records then the royalty shall be 50% of the normal rate and if the Artist be a duo, then the total royalty payable shall be halved before being divided equally between the Artist and the Company.

6. THE Artist hereby authorises the Company to pay any sum due to him into a numbered Swiss bank account, the number of which shall not be divulged to the Artist for reasons of security.

7. THE Artist shall be solely liable for all expenses incurred by the Company in the production, manufacture, distribution and advertising of all Recordings produced by the Company during the term hereof, and in the event of the Artist becoming bankrupt then this agreement shall be binding upon not only his successors but also his friends, relatives and the Official Receiver.

8. IN the event of the Company being unable to get money due to it out of any foreign country then the Artist undertakes to go and get it personally.

9. THE Artist warrants that he has not taken any independent legal advice on the terms hereof. The Artist warrants that he clearly understands this agreement even if he doesn't and further undertakes not to discuss the terms hereof with any other party particularly Private Eye and certain Sunday newspapers.

IN WITNESS WHEREOF etc. etc.

71

QUICK REFERENCE

INSTANT GUIDE TO ROYALTIES

A summary of the royalties and terms which can be expected from Publishers, Record Companies, Managers and Agents.

Publishing contracts

Pay:

10% for *all* U.K. sheet music sales (pro-rata in music books).

50% of all record royalties from U.K. (which the record company pays to the publisher at 6¼% of retail prices less VAT) (*ie* around 2p for you per side of a single and from 0.16p up to about 2p per L.P. track generally).

6/12ths of performing fees (join PRS and get these, including the foreign performing fees which you wouldn't get as a non-member, direct instead of through the publisher). Under £1 to several pounds for radio broadcasts, tens of pounds or more on network T.V. Remember, sampling operates with some local radio. Duration is important.

25% of overseas record royalties.

50% of miscellaneous (half of everything else the publisher gets)

Notes
1. Royalties are paid on 100% of record and sheet music sales, no deductions.
2. You *never* pay a publisher to print or record your song.
3. A "blanket" contract should not last more than five years and ideally should include a provision for you to have back songs which the publisher doesn't want during the agreement.
4. You can get by without a publisher, but you'd probably lose out in the end, and you'd certainly give yourself a lot of work.

Record contracts

For an unknown act around 5%-8% of retail price or "royalty base price" in the absence of a recommended retail price, which is wholesale price plus an average dealer mark-up (around 25-35%). Half this percentage for foreign sales, budget LP's possibly also for cassettes.

Notes
1. Royalties are paid on 90% or less of actual sales.

2. The Record Company may recover its recording costs before paying you on sales of a record.
3. These royalties may not look much, but they're quite normal for new artists.
4. Try to get as short a contract as possible (say one year plus one year plus one year, never over five altogether).
5. Remember you should continue to be paid on sales of your records after you've long since gone to another company.
6. Don't unwittingly give away your song-writing or other rights under the record contract.
7. Remember the record company generally doesn't guarantee to release your records (an independent producer simply can't) but he should guarantee to record a certain number of songs per year.

Management Contracts

Managers' commissions vary enormously. 20% of all earnings from the entertainment business is not unreasonable. An agent ought to get around 10% to 15% of fees for engagements he secures for you. Sometimes he collects the fee and pays you, sometimes you collect and pay his commission to him.

Notes
1. Once you begin to have some success you will need your own accountant (not one recommended by your manager, preferably)
2. Don't give away too much control of your career for too long to a non-professional manager.
3. Look twice at any guaranteed large earnings. You may never get them.
4. If you're in a group and then leave, you're almost certainly still bound as an individual to all the contracts you or your manager have signed. If you join a group who already have contracts you will probably be required to become bound by them as well.
5. Most management contracts cover all aspects of the music business. If you want a manager to negotiate for you and to collect on your behalf from publishers, record companies, agents, film companies, B.B.C. etc. then fine, but if not then a simple letter giving him a percentage of

certain earnings from specific contracts which he has secured for you might be much more satisfactory from your point of view, though the manager concerned may not agree to this.

Finally . . . try not to sign the first deal you're offered if you can see, having read this book, that it's not a good one. Don't be led to think that the company concerned is doing you a huge favour by signing you up. If you really have enough talent to make a good living (or a fortune) in the music business you'll get a better deal elsewhere. Keep your head screwed on, and good luck.

FURTHER READING
AND USEFUL ADDRESSES

At the end of most books you will find a bibliography, giving the names, writers and publishers of other books on the subject. In this case there is no further reading which we can recommend if you wish to go further into the why's and wherefore's of music business contracts without plunging you into heavy discussions on aspects of the Copyright Act, Performers' Protection Acts etc. Instead of this, and of great value by way of familiarising yourself with the British (and overseas) music business is the reading of ordinary periodicals from week to week. As well as telling you what the current singles and l.p. chart movements are, these will give you a good broad picture of which artists and writers and companies are doing what.

The most familiar music weeklies are the NME (New Musical Express), which contains good thoughtful reviews, articles etc. as does Melody Maker, which has the best gig guide, small ads etc. Sounds is very good on the heavy metal scene, and the glossy tabloid Record Mirror caters well for fans of current chart acts. They all have charts, features, news items, reviews and so on, and represent good value for money. Just reading the advertisements will give you a very good idea of who's doing what in the business! There is also the very successful fortnightly magazine Smash Hits, which reproduces lyrics from current hit songs but also has articles etc. aimed mainly at younger readers.

Here is a list of some of the newspapers and magazines comprising the British "Musical Press" plus addresses. These should be available (or may be ordered through) most newsagents. Also included are Radio/TV stations and other useful addresses.

Billboard,
7 Carnaby Street,
London W1.

Black Echoes,
113 High Holborn
London WC1.

Black Music & Jazz Review,
153 Praed Street,
London W2.

Blues & Soul,
153 Praed Street,
London W2.

Broadcast Magazine,
32-34 Great Marlborough Street,
London W1.

Cashbox Magazine,
Flat Six,
196 Sussex Gardens,
London W2.

Classical Music Magazine,
52a Floral Street,
London WC2.

Country Music People,
128a Lowfield Street,
Dartford,
Kent.

Entertainers News,
Central Chambers,
Market Square,
Wellington,
Telford,
Shropshire.

Gramophone,
177-9 Kenton Road,
Harrow,
Middlesex.

Irish Music Scene,
Bunbeg,
Letterkenny,
Co. Donegal,
Eire.

Kerrang!,
40 Long Acre,
London WC2.

Melody Maker,
Berkshire House,
168-173 High Holborn,
London WC1.

Music & Video Week,
40 Long Acre,
London WC2.

New Musical Express,
3rd Floor,
5-7 Carnaby Street,
London W1.

Record Mirror,
40 Long Acre,
London WC2.

Smash Hits,
Lisa House,
52-55 Carnaby Street,
London W1.

Sounds,
40 Long Acre,
London WC2.

The Stage & Television Today,
47 Bermondsey Street,
London SE1.

Studio Sound & Broadcast Sound
Magazines,
Link House,
Dingwall Avenue,
Croydon,
Surrey.

BBC Radio Stations

BBC Radio (1, 2, 3 & 4),
Broadcasting House,
Portland Place,
London W1.

Local Radio – BBC

BBC Local Radio Headquarters,
Henry Wood House,
London W1.

BBC Radio Brighton,
Marlborough Place,
Brighton,
Sussex.

BBC Radio Bristol,
PO Box 194,
Bristol,
Avon.

BBC Radio Cambridgeshire,
Broadcasting House,
Hills Road,
Cambridge,
Cambs.

BBC Radio Cleveland,
PO Box 194,
91-93 Linthorpe Road,
Middlesborough,
Cleveland.

BBC Radio Cornwall,
Malpas Road,
Truro,
Cornwall.

BBC Radio Cumbria,
Hilltop Heights,
London Road,
Carlisle,
Cumbria.

BBC Radio Derby,
56 St. Helen's Street,
Derby.

BBC Radio Devon,
St. David's Hill,
Exeter,
Devon.

BBC Radio Furness (Radio
Cumbria),
Broadcasting House,
Hartington Street,
Barrow-in-Furness,
Cumbria.

BBC Radio Guernsey,
Commerce House,
Les Banques,
St. Peter's Port,
Guernsey,
Channel Islands.

BBC Radio Humberside,
63 Jameson Street,
Hull,
Humberside.

BBC Radio Jersey,
Broadcasting House,
Rouge Bouillon,
St. Helier,
Jersey,
Channel Islands.

BBC Radio Lancashire,
King Street,
Blackburn,
Lancashire.

BBC Radio Leeds,
Broadcasting House,
Woodhouse Lane,
Leeds,
W. Yorkshire.

BBC Radio Leicester,
Epic House,
Charles Street,
Leicester,
Leics.

BBC Radio Lincolnshire,
Radion Buildings,
Newport,
Lincoln,
Lincs.

BBC Radio London,
PO Box 4LG,
35a Marylebone High Street,
London W1.

BBC Radio Manchester,
PO Box 90,
New Broadcasting House,
Oxford Road,
Manchester.

BBC Radio Medway,
30 High Street,
Chatham,
Kent.

BBC Radio Merseyside,
55 Paradise Street,
Liverpool,
Merseyside.

BBC Radio Newcastle,
Crestina House,
Archbold Terrace,
Newcastle-upon-Tyne,
Tyne & Wear.

BBC Radio Norfolk,
Norfolk Tower,
Surrey Street,
Norwich,
Norfolk.

BBC Radio Northampton,
PO Box 1107,
Northampton,
Northants.

BBC Radio Nottingham,
York House,
Mansfield Road,
Nottingham,
Notts.

BBC Radio Oxford,
242-254 Banbury Road,
Oxford,
Oxon.

BBC Radio Sheffield,
Ashdell Grove,
60 Westbourne Road,
Sheffield,
S. Yorkshire.

BBC Radio Solent,
South Western House,
Canute Road,
Southampton,
Hants.

BBC Radio Stoke-on-Trent,
Conway House,
Cheapside,
Hanley,
Stoke-on-Trent,
Staffordshire.

BBC Radio WM (West Midlands),
PO Box 206,
Birmingham,
W. Midlands.

Commercial Radio

Radio Aire,
PO Box 362,
51 Burley Road,
Leeds,
W. Yorkshire.

Beacon Radio,
PO Box 303,
267 Tettenhall Road,
Wolverhampton,
W. Midlands.

BRMB Radio,
PO Box 555,
Radio House,
Aston Road North,
Aston,
Birmingham,
W. Midands.

Capital Radio,
Euston Tower,
London NW1.

Cardiff Broadcasting Company,
Radio House,
West Canal Wharf,
Cardiff,
S. Glamorgan.

Centre Radio,
Granville House,
Granville Road,
Leicester,
Leics.

Chiltern Radio,
Chiltern Road,
Dunstable,
Bedfordshire.

Radio City,
PO Box 194,
8-10 Stanley Street,
Liverpool,
Merseyside.

Radio Clyde,
Ranken House,
Blythswood Court,
Anderston Cross Centre,
Glasgow,
Scotland.

County Sound,
PO Box 7,
8 The Flower Walk,
Guildford,
Surrey.

Devon Air Radio,
The Studio Centre,
35-37 St. David's Hill,
Exeter,
Devon.

Downtown Radio,
PO Box 293,
Kiltonga Industrial Estate,
Newtownards BT23 4ES,
N. Ireland.

Essex Radio,
Radio House,
20 Clifftown road,
Southend-on-Sea,
Essex.

Radio Forth,
Forth House,
Forth Street,
Edinburgh,
Scotland.

Gwent Broadcasting,
c/o Tregarn House,
Tregarn Road,
Langstone,
Newport,
Gwent.

Radio Hallam,
PO Box 194,
Hartshead,
Sheffield,
S. Yorkshire.

Hereward Radio,
114 Bridge Street,
Peterborough,
Cambs.

London Broadcasting Company,
Communications House,
Gough Square,
London EC4.

Marcher Sound/Sain-y-Gororau,
Po Box 238,
Wrexham,
Clwyd.

Mercia Sound,
Hertford Place,
Coventry,
W. Midlands.

Metro Radio,
Radio House,
Long Rigg,
Swalwell,
Newcastle-upon-Tyne,
Tyne & Wear.

Moray Firth Radio,
PO Box 271,
Inverness,
Scotland.

Northside Sound,
1 St. Columb's Court,
Londonderry BT48 6PT,
N. Ireland.

North Sound,
45 Kings Gate,
Aberdeen,
Scotland.

Radio Orwell,
Electric House,
Lloyds Avenue,
Ipswich,
Suffolk.

Pennine Radio,
PO Box 235,
Pennine House,
Forster Square,
Bradford,
W. Yorkshire.

Piccadilly Radio,
127-131 The Piazza,
Piccadilly Plaza,
Manchester.

Plymouth Sound,
Earl's Acre,
Alma Road,
Plymouth,
Devon.

Red Rose Radio,
PO Box 301,
St. Paul's Square,
Preston,
Lancashire.

Saxon Radio,
Electric House,
Lloyds Avenue,
Ipswich,
Suffolk.

Severn Sound,
PO Box 388,
Old Talbot House,
67 Southgate Street,
Gloucester,
Glos.

Signal Radio,
Winton House,
Stoke Road,
Stoke-on-Trent,
Staffordshire.

Swansea Sound,
Victoria Road,
Gowerton,
Swansea,
W. Glamorgan.

Radio Tay,
PO Box 123,
Dundee,
Scotland.

Radio Tees,
74 Dovecot Street,
Stockton-on-Tees,
Cleveland.

Radio Trent,
29-31 Castle Gate,
Nottingham,
Notts.

Radio 210,
PO Box 210,
Reading,
Berkshire.

Two Counties Radio,
5-7 Southcote Road,
Bournemouth,
Hants.

Radio Victory,
PO Box 257,
247 Fratton Road,
Portsmouth,
Hants.

Radio West,
PO Box 963,
Watershed,
Canons Road,
Bristol,
Avon.

West Sound,
Radio House,
54a Holmston Road,
Ayr,
Scotland.

Wiltshire Radio,
Old Lime Kiln Studio,
High Street,
Wootton Bassett,
Swindon,
Wilts.

Radio Wyvern,
5-6 Barbourne Terrace,
Worcester,
Heref. & Worcs.

Others

Radio Luxembourg,
38 Hertford Street,
London W1.

Manx Radio,
PO Box 219,
Broadcasting House,
Douglas,
Isle of Man.

RTE Radio 1 & 2,
Radio Centre,
Radio Telefis Eireann,
Montrose,
Dublin 4,
Eire.

TV – BBC

London:
Television Centre,
Wood Lane,
London W12.

Scotland:
Broadcasting House,
Queen Margaret Drive,
Glasgow,
Scotland.

Wales:
Broadcasting House,
Llantrisant Road,
Llandaff,
Cardiff,
S. Glamorgan.

Northern Ireland:
Broadcasting House,
Ormeau Avenue,
Belfast,
N. Ireland.

TV – Commercial

Anglia,
Anglia House,
Norwich,
Norfolk.

Border,
Television Centre,
Carlisle,
Cumbria.

Central Independent,
Central House,
Broad Street,
Birmingham,
W. Midlands.

Channel,
Television Centre,
St. Helier,
Jersey,
Channel Islands.

Channel Four,
60 Charlotte Street,
London W1.

Grampian,
Queen's Cross,
Aberdeen,
Scotland.

Granada,
Granada TV Centre,
Manchester.

HTV Wales,
Television Centre,
Cardiff,
S. Glamorgan.

HTV West,
Television Centre,
Bath Road,
Bristol,
Avon.

London Weekend,
South Bank Television Centre,
Kent House,
Upper Ground,
London SE1.

Scottish,
Cowcaddens,
Glasgow,
Scotland.

Television South,
Television Centre,
Northam,
Southampton,
Hants.

Television South West,
Derry's Cross,
Plymouth,
Devon.

Thames,
306-315 Euston Road,
London NW1.

Tyne Tees,
Television Centre,
City Road,
Newcastle-upon-Tyne,
Tyne & Wear.

Ulster,
Havelock House,
Ormeau Road,
Belfast,
N. Ireland.

Yorkshire,
Television Centre,
Leeds,
W. Yorkshire.

Miscellaneous

Association of Professional
Recording Studios Ltd.,
23 Chestnut Avenue,
Chorleywood,
Herts.

British Academy of Songwriters,
Composers & Authors,
148 Charing Cross Road,
London WC2.

British Phonographic Industry
Ltd.
273 Regent Street,
London W1.

British Federation of Folk Clubs,
Cecil Sharp House,
2 Regent's Park Road,
London W1.

Country Music Association Inc.,
Suite 3,
52 Haymarket,
London SW1.

Music Publishers' Assoc. Ltd.,
7th Floor,
Kingsway House,
103 Kingsway,
London WC2.

Mechanical Copyright Protection
Society Ltd.,
41 Streatham High Road,
London SW16.

Musicians' Union,
60-62 Clapham Road,
London SW9.

Performing Rights Society Ltd.,
29-33 Berners Street,
London W1.

Phonographic Performance Ltd.,
Ganton House,
14 Ganton Street,
London W1.

British Academy of Songwriters,
Composers & Authors,
148 Charing Cross Road,
London WC2.

GLOSSARY OF TERMS

Here's an alphabetical list of some of the words and phrases which you may come across in the music business. If a word is not defined here you may well find it in the general index.

A & R Man
Artist and Repertoire manager of a record company. He decides which artists on his company's roster record which songs.

Advances
Payments made to writers and artists which generally do not have to be paid back (non-returnable) but which will be recovered by the company from royalties due to the artist, writer etc. i.e. he won't get anything until the royalties he would have got equal the advance payment.

Advance Pressings
A couple of hundred advance pressings, sometimes more, are made of new records, as well as the normal initial pressings for general sale. The advance pressings — marked with a large 'A' and often with a different coloured label are sent to radio disc jockeys or their producers, reviewers for the musical and national press etc.

Arrangers
This term can be used of writers or singers who make arrangements or adaptations of traditional music. Generally in the music business it refers to people who take down music from records for printing, who prepare scores for recording sessions, broadcasts, dance bands and so forth. Some larger companies employ their own full-time arrangers.

Ayants Droit
The owner(s) of the rights. Can mean the original owners (writer and publisher of a song) or new owners (lyric writer and sub-publisher).

Band Calls
Rehearsals for solo acts with the club band at a particular venue. You need to give the band the music you want, and will have to drop from your act, if asked, any song which an act higher up the bill wishes to use. This tends not to apply to rock singers, but to cabaret artists.

Band Parts
Copies of music arranged for brass or other military bands. The demand for these is sufficiently small that few songs are arranged in this way by their publishers for sale and often the band using the song will make their own arrangement with the permission of the publisher and send it to the publisher to have the correct copyright line added.

Blankets
The term used for exclusive (all covering — hence 'blanket') agreements that continue for a period of time.

Bootlegged Records
The dictionary will say that 'Bootlegger' is someone who smuggles alcoholic liquor often concealed in the leg of a high boot — hence 'bootleg'. Today's bootlegger in the music industry can be seen (if he's careless) lurking backstage or in a nearby seat with a microphone and cassette recorder. The microphone used by the smart bootlegger will be clipped to his pocket like a fountain pen and the recorder will be in a case or bag or hidden beneath his coat. His purpose is to tape you 'live' and eventually have made available illicit LP's of your performances reaping him sometimes large financial reward (if you're successful and the songs you performed you have not actually 'recorded' before) for which no artist or copyright royalties are paid. Bootleggers themselves often escape the punishment of the law for it's the sellers that attract attention and retribution. If caught in the act at concerts bootleggers invariably suffer loss or damage to their equipment and often physical assault also.

Breakers
Records 'bubbling under' the charts with sales increasing but not yet enough to push the record into the charts.

Bullet
Mark shown against records making good progress up the USA 'Billboard' trade magazine's weekly charts.

Charts

The best-selling lists of singles and LP's (sometimes sheet music also) as published in the musical press. In the UK the most comprehensive of these is compiled by a leading market research company for the BBC and appears in Music and Video Week although other papers publish their own and there are specialist charts in the specialist and some of the general music papers and magazines for best selling soul, blues, country & western, jazz, classical, and folk LP's or singles. The Music and Video week chart consists of the top 100 singles and LP's, although the lower positions are none too reliable as the chart is compiled from samples of the sales in just a few hundred record shops up and down the country. In the USA 100 singles and 200 LP's are listed. See also under "Crossover".

Collecting Societies

In the UK this term covers the PRS who collect all the performing fees and the MCPS who collect a lot but not all of the mechanical (record) royalties. In France the societies are known as SACEM and SDRM, in Germany the society is GEMA, and in Scandinavia NCB. They do in fact exist in most countries but the names of many are unlikely to reach your ears until you have been in the business for some time. In the USA an organisation called Harry Fox Office collects mechanical royalties, whilst most of the performing fees are collected by two large societies, ASCAP (American Society of Composers, Authors and Publishers) and BMI (Broadcast Music Inc.). Because of this dual situation most USA publishers have a BMI member company and also an ASCAP member company so that songs which they acquire can be fed into either. There is little to choose between them, but a UK or other non-USA writer's songs will more often than not be put by the American sub-publisher into BMI.

Compact Discs

Compact discs (CD's) were launched in a blaze of publicity at the start of 1983. A 7" one-sided disc can contain a whole LP's worth of music, and as it is "read" by a laser beam dirt and scratches do not affect the sound quality. Until most home music centres are fitted with CD decks, both the hardware and the software are likely to remain expensive. As a writer or artist you should be aware that royalties on CD sales will probably not be based on the price of the CD but on say 150% of the price of the ordinary LP equivalent, which is much lower. The superb sound quality possible with CD's of digitally recorded music unfortunately makes it possible for good pirated copies to be made by dubbing straight from the disc.

Commission

The term used to describe the Manager's or Agent's percentage of your earnings.

Compulsory Licence

The right to issue recordings provided that the usual formalities have been completed but provided also that recordings of the song have been released before, i.e. not the first recording.

Container Allowance

Permits record companies to deduct a further percentage (up to 20%) before paying artist royalties. It covers cost of sleeves or cassette/cartridge containers. In some instances mechanical (copyright) royalties are also calculated after a container allowance deduction has been made. A picture-disc LP on coloured vinyl with a gatefold sleeve, lyric sheet and colour poster insert clearly justifies some deduction, but there should be no deduction for an ordinary release.

Contract Year

Used in contracts for a year commencing with the date of the contract and not January 1st.

Controlled Compositions

This refers to a system imposed by USA record companies to ensure that their copyright and artist royalties together do not exceed a certain amount on records where the artist is also the writer. The artist's contract will state that, if his publisher holds out for more than a certain royalty per track then the excess will be deducted from the artist royalty. This is because the USA royalty is subject to negotia- tion, whereas in the UK the statutory 6¼% royalty on retail selling price less tax is fixed except that publishers can, but seldom do, ask for more on the very first release of a song.

Copyist

This is someone generally working with an arranger, who makes neat and easily legible copies of music for various uses from the arranger's draft.

Counterfeits

These are records or videos illegally re-recorded from the original releases or the Master Tapes and pressed up to look exactly like the genuine article, but without any royalties having been paid. These are sold much cheaper to unsuspecting or opportunist dealers, and it is virtually impossible even for the record or video companies concerned to tell them apart, making it hard to find and prosecute counterfeiters.

Covers

Another recorded version of a song originally meaning a copy version but often used to describe all recordings other than the first.

Coupling Right

A clause in a recording contract giving the company the right, without further reference to the artist, to include tracks from one LP/tape on another compilation. Payment on a pro-rata basis is automatic.

Crossover

Apart from being a hi-fi term, this is mainly used to describe records from the specialist charts, soul, independent, country etc. which become hits on the main charts. The specialist charts are generally compiled from sales of records in certain shops dealing mainly in those types of records.

Custom Pressing

The service (expensive) offered by some record manufacturers of pressing just a small quantity of records privately or for sale (i.e. under about 1,000).

Cut-off Periods

Some record companies, publishers and other bodies operate

cut-off periods whereby your statement of money earned in say July-December may actually be cut-off at November and therefore not include some big pre-Christmas sales which you may have been expecting. You will of course get them in the Jan-June statement, which itself may be cut-off at the end of May.

Dealers

The usual term for record shops. There are roughly 7,000 in the U.K. of varying sizes, and many "outlets" such as petrol stations and supermarkets, where impulse buying keeps sales up on budget LP's and cassettes. Most acquire their stocks from "one-stops" who keep stocks of product from most record companies. Some of these actually decide which records should go to certain outlets and "service" them exclusively, usually with middle of the road records. By using one-stops a record shop can order records from different companies at only a fraction more than the normal wholesale price, thus saving time and avoiding record company delivery charges which are added to small orders. In the USA similar companies are known as rack jobbers.

Direct Injection

Plugging an electric instrument, e.g. bass guitar, straight into the mixing desk in a recording studio, instead of recording it into a microphone in front of an amplifier speaker in the studio.

Doubling

Playing more than one instrument at a session, performance etc.

Drop-in

Re-recording part of a track of a recording in a studio, commencing part of the way through without having to start from the beginning.

Dubbing

Re-recording from tape to tape, record to tape or tape to record. BBC pays a nominal dubbing fee for the re-recording of music to be used in its programmes.

Easy Listening

Term used by the USA press especially, to describe 'middle of

the road' music by artists such as Perry Como, Mike Sammes Singers etc.

Exported Records

Sometimes treated as regards royalties as local sales and sometimes as sales in the country of destination. It depends upon the agreement your publisher has with the recording company insofar as copyright royalties are concerned and, with your contract with the recording company, with regard to artist royalties. The artist contract may well say that such are treated

as foreign sales (low rate) or local sales (high rate) or may even spell out the royalty actually for any exports of your recordings.

Facsimile Concession

Permits record companies to place the name of the copyright owner (the publisher, generally) in print on the record labels. A record company without Facsimile Concession will have to buy stamps from the copyright owner and affix them on the label or sleeve. These stamps are often seen on old 78rpms but nowadays only on imported

records or the releases of small companies.

Fixer

Someone who acts as an agent for session musicians and brings the required musicians together, usually for broadcasts or recordings.

Flimsies

Very thin records usually 7" given away free with advertising material and the like. Songs used on them attract a royalty via MCPS which however, is very low. Nevertheless it can amount to hundreds of pounds on some 'giveaway' flimsies by virtue of the enormous numbers produced.

Folk Song

Often used instead of 'Traditional' to describe a Country song that is not copyright. Also often used in connection with 'folky' style songs which may well be copyright and fully protected.

Freebies

These are generally records distributed free to members of the public who subscribe to record mail order organisations and the like. Songs are usually included in these by special arrangement with MCPS and at a minimum rate.

Ghosting

The practice of having experienced musicians playing behind a band on stage without being seen, or playing instead of a group at a recording session just in case the regular group members should make a mistake, which could be costly in studio time wasted.

Grading

The Performing Right Society Ltd. grade songs in accordance with the amount of original material contained. An arrangement of a wholly Traditional/Public Domain song or traditional music with original words, or traditional words (e.g. a Shakespeare poem) with original music will be Downgraded. Affects performing fee income only.

Grand Rights

No legal or clear definition. Often taken as the 'Dramatico Musical Performance right' in connection with songs used in musical stage plays and the like.

Hyping

Exaggerating the merits of a record or artist. Usually this refers to chart-rigging – record companies buying their own records from shops which they believe are making "returns" to the chart compilers or sending quantities of free copies of records to those shops in the hope that they will try harder to sell them or else in the hope of a "you scratch my back . . ." relationship with the shop concerned. This has been widespread in the past, but a company doing this risks having its records removed from the chart.

Imported Records

First read 'exported records' and apply the reverse. If your recording has gone out to the USA and back again on an imported American LP say, then you would be cross if the artist royalty were calculated on the foreign rate (generally half the UK rate) and if you were paid by your company once it had received the money from the USA company months or years later, but this may be perfectly all right under your contract.

The importer in many instances is often the record company who owns the recording locally but prefers to test the market with a few imports before going to the expense of pressing and releasing the recording himself. Your local publisher (or the local mechanical rights society) may or may not collect copyright royalties on imported discs for often they have been paid in the country of export. E.E.C. rules make it difficult to prevent low-priced imported records and tapes being sold in UK record shops at a higher profit margin than British pressings, but the British Phonographic Industry (the trade body of the record companies) and the MCPS have been successful in clamping down on this.

Jingles

The short catchy music or theme used in television, radio and film commercials. Some of these such as "I'd Like To Teach The World To Sing" can become enormous hits given new words.

Lease Tape Deal

An agreement between an independent producer of a Master Tape and a recording company actually in the business of selling records to the public. The independent producer leases his tape to the record company.

Library Records

A recording in the catalogue of a background music ('Mood') record company. These are used, generally, to give a documentary or newsreel background atmosphere but can feature in television commercials and major cinema productions.

The Composers of such music are usually well and truly established people in the music business. Often they are very serious writers indeed. Not 'serious' meaning necessarily composers of symphonic works etc. (although many such composers do indeed write for these libraries) but rather writers who are highly professional, whether as Jazz, Pop or Classical people, and who are able to accept a commission to compose a good and complete musical work of a certain duration and specified instrumentation without too much trouble. The terms of acquisition of such music (they are hardly ever songs, with words) are virtually the same as those for the ordinary songwriter. In these instances the company acquiring the rights, although it produces records and tapes does not release them for sale to the public and although acquiring rights normally held by a music publisher, hardly ever actually prints music editions. Most big music publishers have a Library division even if they do not have an actual commercial recording company offshoot.

Markets

Generally used to describe places in the world where music is used.

Masters, Master Tapes

Finished recordings of sufficient quality for records to be pressed up from them. The word is not used in respect of a completed

demonstration tape unless it is intended for commercial release.

Matrix, Matrices
Another name for masters.

M.D. (Musical Director)
Co-ordinator of the music in plays, musicals, television programmes, films, recording sessions etc. and generally the leader of the band or orchestra performing.

Mechanicals
The royalties payable to the owners of the copyright in a song on a recording and earned by the sales of the records.

Mechanical Reproduction
Any sort of sound record.

Mechanical Restriction
The right of a copyright owner to prevent, until it suits him, the first release of a recording of his song.

Merchandising
Term used to describe the making of goods associated with the name or effigy of an artist.

MIDEM
An annual gathering in winter in the South of France for music industry executives from around the world to do business, sell and acquire songs and recordings etc. There are similar gatherings in the Western Hemisphere as well as conventions to debate matters of worldwide importance to the music industry.

Mixing
This is what the engineer does in a recording studio during a session on the mixer or mixing desk.

Mood Music
Music used in films, commercials etc. (see Library Records).

Non-Member
Usually used to describe the status of a songwriter vis-a-vis a performing right society. A non-member may well lose performing fees unless he has joined such a society.

Orchestrations
Copies of songs arranged for the whole or part of an orchestra. These are very expensive to produce, and whereas they were once considered essential to launch a new song they are now very rarely made by publishers themselves, although bands and orchestras make their own with the publishers' permission and some small private firms are also licensed by publishers to make and sell small quantities.

Parody
Generally humorous versions of songs. The original lyrics are partly or wholly changed to make a comedy version. Some of these can become very big hits.

Payola
An American term for the practice of record companies, publishers etc. bribing disc jockeys or radio producers to broadcast certain records. Broadcasting authorities and companies set rules to determine where reasonable business relations, lunches and small gifts end and payola begins.

Performing Fees
Fees earned by broadcast or other performance of music.

Pirates
Not to be confused with Bootleggers. Pirates abound in countries where copyright is not rigidly enforced. The pirate usually gets a record or video cassette and makes further low quality copies from it without authority. Pirate record labels are usually blank except for the artist's name and song titles. Video cassettes are more often counterfeits – looking just like the original. In some countries books, including songbooks, are also pirated and counterfeited. Pirating is particularly rife in the Far East.

Plays
In the music business this usually means not drama but individual performances of one song, usually a broadcast of a recording.

Play List
Associated with radio stations. The various programme executives meet weekly to hear new record releases and decide whether they are suitable for including in programmes and also decide which records should be removed from the previous list. The principle day time shows which are largely composed of songs from the play list, or the current charts in the absence of a play list are sometimes known as strip shows, because of the way they are put together.

Plugs
Important radio/television broadcast of a recording or live performance.

Power of Attorney
This is the right, given by artists to record companies and managers and by writers to publishers, to take action on their behalf against infringers, bootleggers and other unlawful users of the work in question.

Pressing Plant
A record factory — granules of vinyl are stamped flat in presses to form the records. Most large record companies have their own which are also used by smaller companies, though there are independent concerns pressing records.

Professional Department
Usual name for the department of a publisher concerned with acquiring and promoting songs.

Promoter
Person or company arranging tours and engagements for artists.

Public Domain
No longer copyright.

Racking
The sale of records and tapes on racks in supermarkets, petrol stations etc.

Reducing
This is the process in a recording studio, done normally on a separate occasion after the recording session has finished, when all the different tracks are 'reduced' each one at the right volume level etc. to produce a finished master tape.

Release (of records)
The major companies generally have a specific date of release for each of their records which is always a Friday in the UK, although often disc jockeys will receive advance copies and be playing the record before its actual release.

Release Sheets
Also known as ''dealer mailings'' these are simply sheets sent to every record shop in the country by most major record distributors every week telling the retailers what records are being released and any good reason why the retailer should be sure to order a supply (i.e. previous

record was number 1, forthcoming tour by artist in certain areas etc.).

Re-Releases
Records released by a company for a second time, having previously been deleted due to low sales, and often now having a different catalogue number from the original release, as against re-activated records which are still in the record company's catalogue and selling slowly and which are simply given some fresh publicity.

Returns
Two meanings. One, unsold records returned by the shop to the distributor. Two, information as to uses of songs, i.e. a BBC return (to the PRS) will show songs used in a particular programme.

Roadies
Road Managers or road crew employed by groups to move the sound equipment from one engagement to another.

Routining
Playing through a song prior to a recording or broadcast or live performance to ensure that the artist knows it perfectly.

Sleeper
A record which becomes a hit months or years after its initial release with no further publicity from the record company.

Sub-Publishing
The right of a publisher to authorise other publishers in foreign countries to publish a song.

Tax Exiles
The high rate of UK tax can be especially harsh on those who earn a large sum of money in a relatively short time, causes a regular flow of writers, musicians and singers from the UK to take up residence in countries with more favourable tax laws. Some, like the USA, are good places in any case to further one's career. Others, like the Channel Islands, are not. Writers, whose earnings from hits tend to be spread over a longer period than recording artists, tend to be less affected by this problem.

Terms
Used in contracts in the singular to describe the length of an agreement and in the plural to describe the actual royalty rates and conditions.

Tracks
As well as its use in phrases like "LP tracks" it is used of the facilities of recording studios and tape recorders. 8-track studios are usually only used for demo recordings, but 16-track and upward can be used for Master Tapes for commercial release. 32-track desks and over are usually computerised.

Traditional
No longer copyright.

Transposing
Altering a song from one key to another.

INDEX